JIM
AND
GEORGE'S
HOME WINEMAKING

A BEGINNER'S BOOK

JIM
AND
GEORGE'S
HOME WINEMAKING

A BEGINNER'S BOOK

EASY, PRACTICAL AND COMPLETE

A - PRINTING CO, NAPA, CALIFORNIA

JIM and GEORGE'S HOME
WINEMAKING
A BEGINNER'S BOOK

Published by;

A - Printing Co.
Post Office Box 5523
Napa, CA 94581 U.S.A.

Originally published 1976, Home Fermenter
Publications
Reprinted three times
Reprinted NFS Publications 1988

Copyright 1992 and 1995 by A - Printing Co,
    First printing 1992
    Second printing 1995, complete revision
    and update

Printed in the United States of America
ISBN 0-9630941-3-0 Softcover

FOREWORD

A lot has changed in home winemaking since this book was first published. The basics are practically the same, but new ideas on how to make great homemade wine have become standard and have been included in the update.

Patrick J. Watkins contributed the update information as he has considerable knowledge on home wine and beermaking. He has taught numerous college classes on home winemaking at the Napa Valley College, and he and Colleen have been in the home wine and beermaking supply business for over a decade. Pat shares a similar thought with the late Jim Weathers on home winemaking. That thought is "Keep it simple."

Proofreading the revision and update of the book was onerously accomplished by Colleen F. Watkins. The ease of reading and understanding was examined; and the graphics upgraded by Carole C. Watkins. Rewriting and revisions were completed by Patrick B. Watkins with the aid of a computer.

In memory
of
Jim Weathers

Jim Weathers became associated with the home wine and beermaking trade in 1972; long before home wine and beermaking became widespread and popular. While in the business he wrote three books, including <u>Jim and George's Home Winemaking</u>. He also wrote numerous magazine articles and held workshops and seminars on wine and beermaking throughout the western United States. His knowledge and ability to communicate started hundreds of new home wine and beermakers on the route to making great wine and beer.

"Wine can almost
make itself

All it needs is a little
help from a friend"

TABLE OF CONTENTS

JIM AND GEORGE'S HOME WINEMAKING A BEGINNER'S BOOK

Is the instruction book used in classes held for individuals new to winemaking, and those taking a refresher course at the

NAPA VALLEY HOME WINEMAKING CENTER

in the

Napa Town and Country Fair grounds
NAPA, CALIFORNIA

HOME WINEMAKING

There is really one, just one purpose for this book. It is to give the beginner a simple way to start making wine. We don't want to impress you with charts, calculations and large numbers of wine terms that have been handed down through the ages. We refer to lees as sediment and much of the time to the "must" as wine, but we feel sure you will know what we are talking about. We are trying to approach winemaking at home in the most direct way, a way that you will enjoy working with.

We feel that our book will prepare you to advance in winemaking, not to become an instant expert. Some people who start with this book will need nothing else. They could care less about the technical end; however they will learn enough to be comfortable in making delicious wines that both they and their friends will enjoy.

We personally believe that winemakers who say that theirs is the only way, are completely wrong. We would rather believe that there is room to learn from many sources. Never have a closed mind about winemaking and never be afraid to use your own common sense. Wine can almost make itself. All it needs is a little help from a friend.

Winemaking at home will not only give you an enjoyable hobby but will save you considerable amounts of money over a period of time.

PROCESSES AND METHODS

This section has been organized so that processes and methods are discussed first, then the ingredients and utensils used. At the end of the text we discuss some of the more common problems in winemaking and, finally winemaking concentrates.

SULFITING YOUR MUST

Wine's worst enemies are wild yeast and bacteria. They are in abundance everywhere. Even your body carries several types. The air carries yeast spores to all parts of our environment and if we do not eliminate them, we stand a good chance of losing an otherwise perfectly sound batch of wine.

Along with sulfiting your must, as we mention in the instructions, washing, rinsing and sanitizing all equipment and some ingredients used is very important. We believe this is the most crucial single procedure in making wine. Your chances of getting a bad batch are very remote if you stick to the sanitary straight and narrow all the way through the winemaking process.

When a crushed campden tablet (which is sodium bisulfite) or potassium metabisulfite powder is dissolved in water and added to the must, a gas is released called SULFUR DIOXIDE, also known as SO2. SO2 is used throughout the food industry to eliminate yeast and bacteria growth, thereby retarding the spoilage of fruits and other foods. Once in its gaseous form, the SO2 will eventually leave the must so long as it is in an open container, but not before the sanitizing job has been accomplished.

You may wonder why the SO2 does not kill the wine yeast. There are two good reasons. One is that cultured wine yeasts are able to live in an environment up to 100 parts per million of SO2 in your must or wine. They are harder to kill with SO2 than wild yeast are. Also, by allowing the must to stand overnight before adding the yeast, the SO2 will have dissipated enough so that it will not affect the cultured yeast.

We recommend the campden tablets in our recipes because they are premeasured and much easier for the beginner to use than the powdered potassium metabisulfite. You will get the same results whichever form you use though, tablets or powder.

If you decide to prepare a sanitizing

12

solution with powder, use one ounce of potassium metabisulfite mixed in an eight ounce cup of water.

The powder solution may be used in recipes where campden tablets are called for, in that ONE TEASPOON of this solution is EQUAL TO ONE CAMPDEN TABLET. ONE TEASPOON OF THIS SOLUTION OR ONE CAMPDEN TABLET WILL INCREASE A GALLON OF LIQUID TO 50 PARTS PER MILLION OF SO2. If you think a little SO2 is OK, and more would be better, you're wrong. Stay with the 50 ppm or you can very easily over sulfite your wine.

There are three main reasons for using potassium metabisulfite (SO2) in winemaking. The most important is to sanitize the wine, thereby eliminating unwanted bacteria and wild yeast. The second is as an anti-oxidant factor, and the third, that SO2 inhibits browning of wine.

If you use a TITRET TEST KIT, which measures the amount of SO2 in wine, you will get a close estimate of the amount of SO2 in your wine. The results of a test will tell you if you have enough, or you need more SO2 in your wine. Titret kits are available at home wine and beer supply stores.

A sanitizing solution of potassium metabisulfite powder or campden tablets will have a pungent odor. Try not to breathe the pungent odor, as it can affect your respiratory system.

YEAST STARTER

The reason we suggest using a starter is that you are just about guaranteed a 100% start of the fermentation of your must with the yeast starter. By growing the yeast in its own special environment it has a chance to become super strong and to multiply itself a thousand fold before being introduced into the must. You will learn how to prepare the starter, and you can use it in your wine recipes.

PREPARATION OF FRUITS AND BERRIES

It is relatively simple to prepare fruits and berries for fermentation. The tools and equipment you use will depend on the size of the batch you plan to make and whether you plan to prepare the fruits by heating or by crushing and pressing. In turn, the method you use will depend in part on whether you plan to ferment the juice only or to ferment both the crushed pulp and juice. The decision you make will usually be determined by whether you want a darker or lighter wine. Also, some fruits give a better flavor by using one method or the other, just as some jams and jellies have a more intense flavor when freezer-made rather than boiled.

If you plan to ferment the juice only, two general methods are available to you, preparation by heating or pressing. If you plan to ferment on the pulp, crushing is the way you will need to go.

In the past, fruits were often heated for sterilization purposes. With campden tablets, and potassium metabisulfite powder available this is no longer necessary. However, people still heat their fruit for a variety of reasons. Some use this procedure just because they like the flavor a stewed fruit imparts in the wine, or just because they'd rather heat than crush.

Whatever the reason, heating the fruit can be accomplished by just stewing it in a pan, or by a more elaborate steaming-extracting process. When using the steaming-extracting process, the fruit is not in boiling water but in a separate compartment above the water. As the heat breaks down the skins of the fruit, the juice flows from the fruit and out a drain into a receiving container. When using this method, the pulp is next squeezed through a filter bag to extract any remaining juice. An important thing to keep in mind in any heat preparation method, is the natural pectic enzyme that would normally eliminate any pectin haze in the wine is itself eliminated by heating. So you have to add pectic enzyme here, but only after heating and cooling the fruit, or what you add will also be destroyed by heat.

Crushing and/ or pressing the fruit, will, as we have mentioned, give you juice only or pulp and juice. It is important to clean the fruit thoroughly with cold water and remove all unripe and unsound portions before these methods are used. For crushing small amounts of fruit, something simple, like a potato masher, will be sufficient.

15

Bigger batches need bigger equipment such as a crusher or a crusher stemmer (a crusher stemmer removes stems and leaves as you crush your fruit or grapes). A large grape or fruit press would also be needed. You can rent or you can buy these through your home beer and wine supply dealer.

When using a press, you will not have to put the pulp through a filter bag, as all the juice should be extracted clean. Note: some fruit, apples and pears for example, need to be crushed before they are pressed.

One last suggestion, it is possible to make a false wine by pressing the fruit, using the juice for one batch and the pulp for another. Another variation on this is to ferment "on the pulp" in the primary stage. Then to separate the juice and pulp by straining, pouring the juice into a carboy (5 gallon water bottle) for the secondary fermentation and starting a new batch with the pulp.

FERMENTING AREA

While fermenting, wine should be kept as close to a constant temperature as possible, and between 65 and 80 degrees. Fermentation will stop if the temperature is too high. Cold fermentation requires lower temperature (see section on cold fermentation). Make sure there are no drafts and if possible keep your fermenting wine off the floor.

RACKING THE WINE

We describe this process thoroughly in the procedure section. Racking is accomplished by siphoning the wine off the lees at the bottom of the gallon jug or five gallon carboy. Lees consist of dead yeast cells and fruit pulp, both of which can impart an off taste to the wine. Quite often, winemakers will complain that they have an unpleasant tasting wine, and during the conversation will reveal that they seldom or never racked their wine. It may be, they did not know or understand the reason behind the process of racking, or they just forgot to do it.

It is very difficult to advise you on just when to rack the wine. The first racking from the primary fermenter to the secondary fermenter can usually be done about five to seven days after you put the yeast in the must; providing however, the fermenting action has slowed down considerably and you believe that after you have racked it into a jug or carboy it won't bubble over the top. (Don't leave the pulp and sediment in the must too long. You can get an off taste from the pulp if left too long in the primary container.) Some fruit and berry wine should be racked after a couple of days, providing the fermentation action has slowed down.

After you have racked the wine into the secondary container, keep an eye on the bottom of the glass container. When the sediment builds up to 1/4 to 1/2 inch deep, it is time to rack. This may occur a few times according to

17

the amount of pulp in your wine. If it does, rack again. Then rack at least every two months until the wine clears. Most wine will clear through racking. <u>Don't forget to rack</u>.

SUGAR WATER (syrup)

Each time you rack your wine you will lose some juice in the process. The amount of juice you lose can be replaced with sugar water. Put three ounces of cane sugar in a measuring cup and fill with water to the one cup level, boil, <u>cool</u>, and add to top off your wine.

CLARIFYING (CLEARING) (FINING) WINE

As we have mentioned, most wines clear satisfactorily during the normal racking process. Sometimes, though, even after racking, a wine will still be hazy or cloudy. What causes this haze? Could it have been prevented or at least eliminated after it occurred?

A cloudy or hazy fruit wine is caused quite often by pectin, a substance most important in jelly and jam making. It can actually solidify and jell in the winemaking process. Some wines heavy with pectin will form globs that may resemble fuzzy animals. This does not hurt the flavor of the wine one bit, but it sure will give a person second thoughts about drinking from a bottle where this "thing" is preserved!

Most fruits have an enzyme just under their skins that will break down pectin. However, as we mentioned, heating fruit to sterilizing it, or not cooling the boiled sterilized water, before adding it to the must will destroy that enzyme.

There is a pectic enzyme on the market that will prevent or eliminate a pectin haze, should it occur. Generally, a recipe will recommend it if the fruit is naturally high in pectin. The best time to introduce the enzyme to the wine is at the very beginning. If you do not use it at first, and you suspect your wine is somewhat hazy, it can be added at any time during the fermentation process. One way to check for pectin haze is to hold a lighted match behind the glass fermenter.

If the wine is clear, the flame will appear vivid and sharp. If a haze is present, the flame will appear fuzzy. One added note: if you do add pectic enzyme to the must during the later fermentation process rather than at the beginning, allow at least two weeks for the haze to settle out before bottling.

If you have used pectic enzyme as directed and your wine is still cloudy, there are several substances available that can be useful. BUT don't rush your wine. Before you use any fining agent, give it time to clear on its own.

One fining agent we have come across is a commercial product with a refined seaweed base called sparkolloid. It works very well with <u>white wines</u>. You can buy sparkolloid in either a powder or tablet form. Don't forget to ask for directions on how to use it. It will clarify where other clearing agents might not.

Gelatin is a popular fining agent. If you use it, be sure to use unflavored gelatin. Gelatin reduces astringency by removing tannin from the wine. It won't work in white wine without tannin. Recommended amount: 2 grams per 5 gallons of wine. Dissolve in 1/2 cup of warm water and let stand until clear. Gently stir it into your wine and let it sit. It may take some time for it to settle to the bottom of your wine, when it does and the wine is clear, rack off the wine.

There is considerable literature on clarifying wine with fining agents and filters. It is also a subject with considerable room for opinion, but the information we have provided should help you through your first few batches. If you need more information on the subject, your home wine and beer supply store people can help you.

BOTTLING WINE

At bottling time, your wine should contain about 25 to 50 parts per million (ppm) of sulfite. If you think the wine is low in sulfite, or you have not added any since you started the primary fermentation, you can add one campden tablet crushed and dissolved in a little water to each gallon of wine before you bottle it. The sulfite acts as a preservative and helps prevent fermentation from restarting in the bottle. (If fermentation was not finished when you bottled.)

Titret kits are very useful just before bottling, as they are used to measure the amount of sulfite in your wine.

Bottling the wine is the last step in the wine making process. Correct and suitable bottling procedures will insure that the wine you have labored so diligently to create will last in good condition until you drink it.

We recommend that you bottle your wine

in the size container that you will find comfortable to consume in one single evening or occasion. 750 ml wine bottles are the most popular size. There is also the 375 ml bottle that is half the size of the 750 ml.

When you fill your bottle with wine, leave some space in the top of the bottle at least the length, and a little more, of the cork you are going to use. A bottle filler is a handy piece of equipment to use, as it leaves the proper amount of space in the neck of the bottle for the cork.

A problem can develop if you decide to store or bottle your wine in a larger container. If you store or bottle it in a one gallon size container or larger, you may find it difficult to drink the total amount at one sitting without a great deal of help.

Aging wine in a larger container is good. Wineries do it all the time. But, they keep their containers full or topped off so that air cannot get to the wine. The wine will age better this way. When the home winemaker starts to draw off the wine, more and more air space is created inside the container, which allows more air to come into contact with the wine and that is bad. During the secondary fermentation stage, and after bottling or storing, exposure to air can be damaging to wine. Air can affect the aroma and taste and cause the wine to oxidize.

CORKS AND CORKERS

Most home winemakers invest in a corker, mainly because it is almost impossible to get a standard wine cork into a wine bottle without one. Most corkers work on the same principle. With the squeeze type, the cork is compressed by the corker and a special plunger drives it into the opening at the top of the bottle. With the wooden and some plastic corkers, the cork is forced down through a tapered hole into the top of the bottle by a plunger. They all work, but we prefer the squeeze type corker. As all corks are larger than the inside neck of the bottle, it seems to us, that with the squeeze type the cork goes into the bottle easier, with less effort on our part.

A 9 X 1 3/4 cork is the standard size wine cork for a 375 and 750 ml wine bottle. All the corks you use should be soaked in an SO2 (potassium metabisulfite) solution for about a 1/2 hour. This is done to sanitize, (don't rinse the corks after soaking) soften, and moisten the corks so they will insert into the bottle. If you don't soak the corks, it is very difficult to insert them into the bottle. Once inside the neck of the bottle, the cork expands instantly and seals the bottle.

After corking, the bottles should stand upright for at least five days. The still wet corks tend to be pushed out by the compressed air that is trapped in the bottle, if they are stored on their sides right after corking. After five days, the bottles should lie on their sides to keep the corks damp so they will not dry out completely and shrink. If the cork shrinks, it can cause the bottle to leak and possibly cause oxidation of the wine.

A standard wine cork should protect your wine for a number of years. For any wine you don't expect to keep more than a year you might want to use a "T" cork. A "T" cork looks just like a T. It is a short cork with a beveled edge and can be inserted into a wine bottle without a corker.

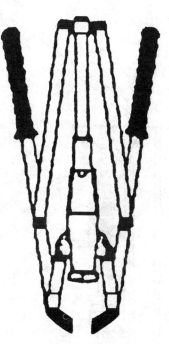

Hand wing corker

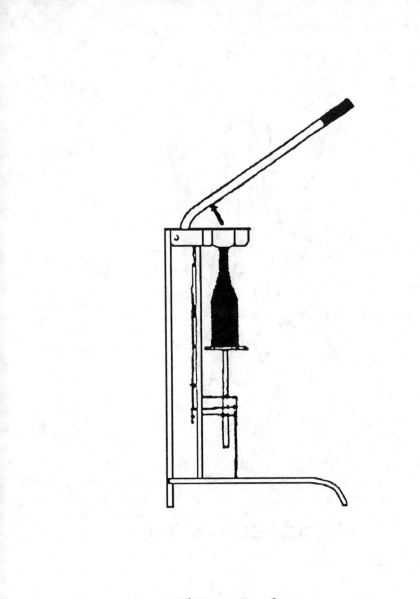

Floor corker

ADDITIVES USED BY HOME WINEMAKERS

One of the several good things about making your own wine is that you know what, if anything, has been added to it and in what amounts.

Additives balance a wine. Keep in mind, that when you balance a wine, you are merely doing a job that nature could not do; either because of a short growing season, too much acid in the soil, or too much or not enough rain. It may be just because a particular variety of fruit is deficient in certain chemicals that otherwise, like grapes, usually have good balance.

ACID AND YOUR WINE

For example, with no acid in wine you would have a very bland tasting wine. Too much acid, and your wine would be too tart. Although acid is very natural in fruit, acid content can vary in the same fruit from season to season.

Suppose you have a growing season cooler than normal, with less sunshine. This causes the fruit to produce less sugar and retain more of the acid at harvest time. Normally, a ripe berry contains seven to ten times less acid than the green fruit, but the short growing season has altered this. So we have a fruit high in acid and short on sugar. The soil and short growing season in the Northwest regularly cause a high acid content in most fruits. The home winemaker in this area usually has to dilute the juice he uses, about two parts juice to one part water.

This brings us to the solution of acid problems: too much natural acid in the fruit, and we dilute the juice. Too little, and we add acids to the juice usually in the beginning. Balancing wines for acid after the wine is finished is the wrong way to approach the problem, although it can be done. The easiest way to determine all this is with an Acid Test Kit. Included in an Acid Test Kit are complete directions for how to use one. However, if just the words "acid test kit" or "acid titration kit" send a chill up your spine, relax. We really recommend to the beginner that you use your sense of taste to develop a feel for over and under acidity in wine before you start to rely entirely on a kit. If you want to make the best wine, though, you will eventually have to learn how to use an acid titration kit to correct the balance of the must (wine) at the beginning.

The acids you will use mostly are citric, malic and tartaric. Citric acid is present in citrus fruits, malic in tree fruits, such as apples, and tartaric in grapes. Generally a recipe will include acid blend, as acid blend is a blend of all three acids.

Acids can be used to balance a finished wine. With experience, you can do this yourself, or you can have an expert do it for you. To raise the acid content in a low-acid finished wine requires tests, the addition of the correct amount of acids and a re-aging period to blend the acids into the wine.

Acids may be reduced in wine with plain boiled and cooled water, but at the same time you are diluting the alcohol content. Really, the only way we would recommend for a beginner to modify a too high or low acid quality in a finished wine, would be by blending one finished wine with another finished wine.

ACID BALANCE

A wine without the proper acid balance will usually be quite tart if high in acid, or bland and lifeless if too low in acid. Also, apart from taste, acids actually help keep wine fresh for years. So a wine with a very low acid level will not keep as long as a correctly balanced wine.

For these reasons, it is most important to learn to use an Acid Titration Kit. Just as it used to be said. "The time to close the barn door is before the horse gets out," the time to balance acids in wine or must is before fermentation begins. So let's learn to do it the right way.

31

We recommend that you use an <u>Acid</u> <u>Titration Kit</u>. It will tell you how much acid your wine has. You then either dilute the must with water to reduce over-acidity, or add acids to raise the acid content. We suggest using acid blend for fruit and tartaric acid for grape wine.

It might help to remember this, one part water to one part juice will lower the acid content 50%. From this, you can almost compute the amount of water you will need to reduce the acid level in your juice. For example, one part water to two parts juice, will reduce the acid content by 25%. To raise the acid level, use this formula: one ounce of acid blend will raise five gallons of juice by .15%. So, one ounce of acid blend in one gallon of juice will raise the acid level by five times, or .75%.

Since some people prefer more acid taste in their finished wine than others, you will need to experiment somewhat, using the basic acid test kit recommendations to guide you. Most kits recommend dry wines, that are to be consumed soon, be .45% to .60%, a red wine you are going to age .65% to .70% and white wine .70% to .80%. Sweet wine should have a broader range because the sweetness tends to mask the acid taste. Sweet wines can be balanced anywhere from .50% to .75%. Test a couple of wines with the kit. Taste the wine first, then make an acid test and find their acid level. With the known standard of the kit, you can now work up or down from these, depending on your individual taste.

WARNING: An **acid test kit** contains **sodium hydroxide**. It is a poison! Be sure to rinse out all the equipment after testing. Place the test kit, and especially the sodium hydroxide, in a safe place where a curious child can't get to it.

ACID TEST KIT

CONTENTS OF KIT:
4 oz. sodium hydroxide 0.100 N (NaOH)
2 drams phenolphthalein (indicator)
250 ml Erlenmeyer flask
10 cc syringe
eye dropper

DIRECTIONS: 1) Fill flask with 2 oz. or 60 cc distilled boiling water. To this add 10 cc juice or wine, mix well. 2) Add 5 drops phenolphthalein (indicator). 3) Now clean the syringe and fill it with 10 cc sodium hydroxide. Slowly add sodium hydroxide to wine or juice in flask, swirling flask continuously until the "End Point" is reached. The "End Point" is that point at which all the acid has been neutralized. The "End Point" for white wine is light pink to orange-pink, and gray-green or brown for red wine. Record the amount of cc sodium hydroxide used. 4) To determine the amount of acid, take the total cc used to reach the "End Point" and multiply by .075. 5) Make sure that the bottles are kept well stoppered when not in use, as both solutions will deteriorate by exposure to air. Wash syringe, eye dropper and flask after use.

ACID TESTING

First take a sample of
the juice with as →
little pulp as possible.

Remove 10 cc of the juice,
add 2 ozs. distilled water,
and put into " testing jar ".

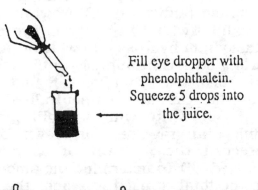

Fill eye dropper with
phenolphthalein.
Squeeze 5 drops into
the juice.

Rinse the syringe and fill
with 10 cc Sodium Hydroxide.

Now start adding the
Sodium Hydroxide 1 cc at
a time, to the juice in the testing jar.
Swirl till "End Point" is reached.

If you are using a red wine, the juice will turn gray green or brown at the "End Point". A white wine will turn orange pink or light pink. Your acid kit will contain instructions on the "End Points", etc.

APPROXIMATE DESIRABLE ACID LEVELS
Red grape wines .65% to .75%
White grape wines .7% to .8%
Fruit wines .6%

To increase the acid add tartaric acid or acid blend. One (1) oz. acid added to 5 gallons of must raises the acid content by .15%.

To decrease the acid content, the best method is to blend the high acid grapes with others known to be low in acid. A much less desirable way to reduce acid would be to add water.

TANNIN

Tannin, usually referred to as grape tannin in wine making, is an uncommon substance found mostly in tea, oak and grapes. It is what gives your iced tea its refreshing bite and wine, its special character. You may not know it when you taste it, but you will certainly know it when no tannin is present.

Tannin is present in tea, oak and grapes, but it is not present in much else. The easiest way to get it for the fruit you are working with is to buy it. It is packaged in very small quantities because not much is needed to be effective. For example, apple wine needs only a 1/4 level teaspoon per gallon. So go easy when using it. Tannin in the refined state is a fine dark powder and looks like instant tea.

You can get tannin into your wine by aging it in an oak barrel; especially a new oak barrel. One problem: Remember, the smaller the batch of wine, the more the wine will be exposed to the sides of the barrel, which can give your wine too strong a tannin and oak flavor.

Another way of introducing tannin and an oak flavor to your wine, is with oak chips, which is a convenient way of doing it. When, by the taste test, you think there is enough flavor, you can remove the oak chips. You can get oak chips and the instructions for using them at home wine and beermaking supply stores.

SUGAR

We can classify sugar as an additive in home winemaking. Most fruits and berries do not have enough natural sugar to produce the amount of alcohol required to preserve the wine. By the time we dilute the juice more, if needed, so that we can reduce the acid content, we would even have less sugar per gallon to produce alcohol. This is the main reason for the addition of sugar. It would be great if we did not have to add sugar, but as you can see, it is often necessary.

It is often difficult for the beginner to decide just what kind of sugar to use to make wine. Any sugar that will ferment into alcohol can be used, but what will ferment best?

Most of us are familiar with cane and beet sugar. These two sugars, both sucrose, will ferment into alcohol, but not readily. Some books on winemaking advise converting sucrose before you introduce it into your must. By converting, they mean changing it into an invert sugar. Invert sugar is a sugar the will readily ferment into alcohol. The natural sugar in grapes is invert sugar; corn sugar is invert sugar.

How do you invert cane or beet sugar? Dissolve the sugar in gently boiling water for a couple of minutes. In the process of converting sugar to alcohol, yeast itself, along with the acid in the fruit, can turn cane or beet sugar to invert sugar. It just does not happen as quickly as if you prepare the sugar ahead of time.

37

The commercial winemaker, in a number of areas around the world, would like to be able to make wine like the home winemaker, as far as sugar goes.   By law, in those areas, the winemaker is allowed to add only a small amount of sugar or none at all.

As a home winemaker, you can add sugar to bring your wine's alcohol up to the percentage that is needed. In most cases grapes in colder climates do not mature with enough sugar to reach ten percent alcohol and we know that we should have enough alcohol to preserve the wine.

Sugaring the must-----is a popular tactic with some European winemakers. However, as we said it is an illegal act in some areas. Some regions in France, such as Beaujolais, may, again by law, add sugar, but only to the amount that it will increase the alcohol strength by no more than two degrees.

In some areas around the world, as we said, the winemaker is not allowed to add sugar or commercial yeast to the wine. He must depend entirely on the dominant yeast that exists in the area. In this case he may not use SO2 because, first, it would kill the natural yeast, and second, it is illegal to introduce any other yeast into the must. If it were not for such laws regarding sugar and yeast, he could adjust the additives when making wine and probably come up with a vintage year, every year.

In California it is a state law that

commercial winemakers may not add sugar to a must that is low in sugar. To get around this law, the winery might add concentrated grape juice to the must to bring the sugar content up to a desired level. Concentrate, of course, is low on water and high on sugar. Usually concentrated juice contains a Brix-balling of 69 degrees, plus or minus 2 Brix. (Keep in mind, that to obtain an alcohol content of 11% we need 21 Brix.)

In other ways, California winemakers have more leeway in their winemaking than do their counterparts in Europe. For instance, most California and Oregon wineries use the same yeast in making wine as the home winemaker.

90 "To the health of the grape" (Honoré Daumier)

WINE YEAST

Yeast is a living organism that feeds on sugar and oxygen, converting it to alcohol and releasing carbon dioxide gas in the process. It is present in the air in hundreds of different strains, some more tolerant to alcohol than others.

In areas like Burgundy, Bordeaux, and Sauterne, France, the predominant yeasts in the air, are those that produce these particular wines. By law, the commercial winemakers in those areas must use the natural yeast only, as it is the one congenial to their particular wines.

The yeast you decide to use is what is under discussion however, and really is a vital factor in making good wine. Of course, you too could make wine by waiting for the yeast in the air and on the fruit to work on the sugar, but we don't recommend it. This is the way home and kitchen wines were made for centuries. Sure, it can make great wine, especially if you live in the wine districts of France; but it can also make

41

very bad wine if you don't, especially if the wrong yeast is dominate in the air.

We suggest that so far as yeast is concerned, you don't push your luck too far. As we said, it is possible to make wine with the yeast that is already present in the air and on the fruit, the natural way, but this is taking a chance. However, if you decide that you want to try making a small batch of wine the natural way, don't sulfite the wine or it will kill the natural yeast.

Instead of taking a chance with natural wild yeast, we suggest eliminating it with SO2 and introducing the commercial wine yeast of your choice.

There are many kinds of commercially packaged wine yeast which definitely lend character to wine, and are a very satisfactory product. Some of the commercial wine yeast available:

PREMIER CUV'EE: Suggested for Chardonnay, Cabernet Sauvignon and Zinfandel, and fruit wines.

MONTRACHET: Suggested for Chardonnay, Cabernet Sauvignon and Zinfandel.

PASTEUR CHAMPAGNE: Suggested for Cabernet Sauvignon, and other reds and whites.

COTE des BLANCS: Suggested for Chenin

Blanc and fruit wines, such as apple, apricot, peach, plum and pear.

PASTEUR RED: Suggested for Cabernet Sauvignon, Zinfandel and various red wines, and Bordeaux style reds.

LALVIN 71 B-1122: Suggested for Concentrates.

LALVIN K1-V-1116: Suggested for Grape and Fruit wine.

We think you should try different wine yeasts to see how you like them. There is more information available that will help you match a particular yeast with the likeliest fruits. Your home winemaking supply store people can make recommendations.

The type of wine yeast we use as an all-purpose wine yeast is Premier Cuv'ee. It is inexpensive, made in the United States and comes in granule form in a 5 gram packet, which is sufficient for one to five gallons of wine. This yeast will generally live in 14% alcohol, and will clear very cleanly after forming a definite sediment on the bottom of the jug or carboy.

When we mention high alcohol contents, by the way, we are not advocating a drink that will get you tipsy. Alcohol acts as a preservative for wine. A homemade wine with an alcohol percentage below 10%, if not drank soon, may have more trouble with spoilage.

When you make any red wine you can use

Premier Cuv'ee or Montrachet as an all purpose wine yeast; whether you are making wine from varietal grapes like cabernet sauvignon, pinot noir or even concord. The Montrachet yeast may have a slightly shorter fermentation period but because of the grapes strong acids and tannin content the faster fermentation does not seem to bother the product.

Champagne yeast can be used for all white wines, whether you use fruit or grapes. This yeast will ferment at temperatures slightly below 60 degrees. At this temperature, the slower fermentation should improve the delicate flavor of white wines.

The most common complaint from beginning winemakers is, "My wine tastes yeasty." "Did I put too much yeast in the must?" This would be highly unlikely. When you prepare a **yeast starter**, (see page 93) with one pack of dry yeast, it grows. By the time the yeast starter has been added to the must, the yeast has grown to the equivalent of many, many packs of yeast. (When you make a yeast starter, add **yeast nutrient** to give the yeast a boost. Also, a nutrient will help the yeast to live in low oxygen situations where normally the yeast would die.)

More probably, a yeasty flavor comes from drinking the wine too soon after it is bottled; before the yeast taste has had a chance to mellow into the whole flavor of the wine. The yeast flavor could also be from not racking cleanly, (picking up too much sediment from the

44

bottom of the fermenter, when you siphon). It could even be caused by unsanitary conditions that permitted other yeast to grow along with the wine yeast.

It may be difficult for a beginner to know for sure if the yeast is working in the must. It may take a few days for the yeast to develop enough fermentation, so that the activity can be detected just by looking at the must. Usually after the yeast has been in the must for two days you can detect fermentation by stirring the must rapidly. This will cause trapped carbon dioxide gas to be released, causing foaming on the top of the must. This is a sure indication that the fermentation has started. Then you can relax knowing that everything is OK.

When using the cold fermentation method it can take a day or two longer before any noticeable fermentation takes place.

55   A Rustic Divinity Carrying Wine Jugs (European, xvi century)

COLD FERMENTATION

To carry out the "cold fermentation" method, you must have the facilities and an area in which to work.

Cold fermentation is a term applied to the process of fermenting a wine at temperatures below the usual 70 to 80 degrees. It is generally believed that a wine fermenting at a lower temperature and a slower pace will yield a better product. Naturally, to ferment at a lower temperature, we are going to need a yeast that will live under the lower temperatures. We have found that the champagne yeast produced in the United States will do this job.

After sulfiting the must, but with the temperature at a low of about 60 degrees F., add the yeast as you normally would. Don't be alarmed if the yeast is not immediately active. It usually takes a little longer for the yeast growth to start. Be sure to transfer the must from the primary to the secondary fermenter as soon as the fermentation slows down, and you feel the

47

secondary fermenter will handle the must without it overflowing through the airlock.

In the cold fermentation process you must plan on at least three months and possibly six months to complete the fermentation process. In this case, you must really keep the temperature controlled within a 5 degree range of your starting temperature, which is usually 60 to 65 degrees. After fermentation has been completed, the aging temperature should be around 55 to 65 degrees.

EXAMPLE OF COLD FERMENTATION

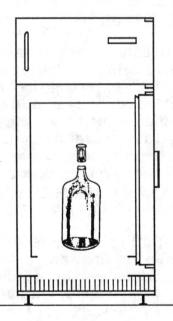

PROBLEMS AND SOLVING THEM

Although we have tried to stress that it is relatively easy to make your own wine, don't let this lull you into a sense that nothing can go wrong, because some things can. What we would like to emphasize is that for almost every problem there is a solution. The difficulty lies in deciding what is the cause of the problem. Identical conditions can arise from widely different causes, calling for completely different solutions. When we know the specific cause for the condition, then certain steps can usually be taken to correct the problem.

STUCK FERMENTATION

A good example of a problem is the situation known as stuck fermentation. We sometimes can figure out the causes of a stuck fermentation because of what happens. For instance, suppose the yeast doesn't start to work within six hours of being added to the must. One of the first possibilities, did you use too much potassium metabisulfite powder or campden tablets? Did you not wait long enough for the SO2 to dissipate from the must before adding the yeast? You can test this by taking a breath right near the must itself. If you can easily detect the odor that you have learned to recognize as SO2, then you have probably discovered the reason for your non-working yeast.

Now the solution! Just stir the must vigorously two or three times, about an hour or so apart, then let it sit overnight. If the yeast has not started fermenting by that time, you can conclude that the yeast was destroyed by the SO2. Prepare another yeast starter, introduce it to the must, and continue to follow the normal steps.

If you didn't use a nutrient, this could definitely be your problem. Always use yeast nutrient. At least one tablet per gallon or one teaspoon of powdered nutrient per gallon will be enough. If it makes you feel any better, you can use a little more without any ill effects. So assuming your must is stuck, and you didn't use any nutrient, mix the proper amount of nutrient in a small amount of water. Add this to the must and stir vigorously.

Another reason for the yeast having difficulty in getting started is that you may be working with a low acid fruit. If you have an **acid test kit**, you can quickly test for this. If not, and you did not make a yeast starter, as we describe (page 93) on making dry wine; then add one half to one teaspoon of acid blend per gallon

50

to the must. This should be with low-acid fruits, most vegetables and flowers. Some fruits that are normally low in acid are pears, figs and dried fruit. Medium acid fruits that can also be low in acid are, apples, apricots, cherries, plums, peaches, some juice concentrates and grapes.

Another cause of stuck fermentation could be the addition of too much sugar, too soon. Yeast needs sugar to live, <u>but not too much at one time</u>! If you are not using a hydrometer (which you should) and you do not know exactly how much sugar you will be needing, go easy. A good rule of thumb is, never add more than two and a half pounds of cane sugar per gallon when starting a batch, unless a recipe calls for it.

The way to detect a stuck fermentation caused by too much sugar is the syrupy quality of the must. One way to solve the problem is to dilute the sugar content using more unsweetened juice. Another way, although not advisable as it can alter the flavor of your finished wine, is to add boiled and cooled water, a little at a time. If you don't have any more unsweetened juice, this may be the only way.

Here again, (if you have one) is where a hydrometer is especially helpful. If your hydrometer reads above 1.125, you have probably added too much sugar to your must. The starting specific gravity for dry wine should be around 1.084 to 1.090, and sweet wine, up to 1.120.

If you have already checked several

possibilities for a stuck fermentation and you keep coming up empty, then check the temperature of the must with a thermometer. Must with an all-purpose yeast should be kept at 65 to 80 degrees F., while yeast in cold fermenting must should be around 55 to 65 degrees. Even then, too low a temperature can cause a stuck fermentation We've said it before and we will say it again--no drafts. Drafts can make the temperature of the wine fluctuate. If you are making, or going to make wine in your garage, and many people do, make sure you make provisions for unseasonable evening chills and cold nights.

A floating thermometer is a good investment. You can put it in your must and leave it there. This way you can tell, almost at a glance just what the temperature of you must is at any given time.

Yeast is a living, growing thing and temperature change, gradual or rapidly either way can seriously damage its growth. Too low a temperature will usually cause it to become dormant, while too high a temperature, above 85 degrees, can kill the yeast. So keep an eye on the temperature of your wine, especially when there is a sudden change in the weather, and make adjustments if necessary.

Now, you have checked for too much potassium metabisulfite, not enough acid, too little nutrient, too much sugar and temperature problems. Still nothing! Whatever the reason, your fermentation is genuinely stuck. So let's try to un-stick it by preparing a new yeast starter and introducing it into the must. As this is the primary stage of fermentation, and it is relatively easy to eliminate causes of stuck must, you should be off and running with an unstuck fermentation.

This can also be done during the secondary fermentation stage. If when using a hydrometer, you find that the specific gravity is well above 1.000, and it has been at the same specific gravity for several days and there is no evidence of fermentation, use a new yeast starter.

You will need a half-gallon jar with a wide mouth. Wash and sanitize it. Prepare a yeast starter that will fill the jar only one quarter full. Let the starter grow for several hours, then remove twice the amount of stuck wine than you have starter from the fermenter, and pour into the starter jar, and cover. Now you will need a secondary container large enough to hold the original must and the new starter. The next day again, do the same thing, adding twice the amount of stuck wine to the newly started must. Each following day, do the same thing until you have introduced all the stuck wine into the new must. If you feel that the fermentation is slowing down at any point, wait a day before adding more stuck wine to the new batch.

AIR (OXYGEN IN YOUR WINE)

Did you ever drink some leftover wine out of a glass "the morning after"? The difference between the wine when you opened it and the wine the next day when you drank it, after being exposed to air for several hours, is something akin to the oxidation that can occur in your carboy as you make your wine. As we have already mentioned, oxygen won't harm during the primary fermentation stage. When you are stirring and aerating the must daily, you are feeding it the oxygen that the yeast must have in the early stages to become strong.

When the wine reaches stage two, (secondary fermentation) however, the time has come to exercise care and caution. As little oxygen as possible should come in contact with your wine. Keep in mind particularly, that every time you rack your wine you are exposing the wine to unwanted oxygen. In our beginning instructions on the first racking we suggested using the primary fermenter as the receiving container, while the sediment was being removed from the jug or carboy; then re-siphoning the wine back into the carboy after cleaning. If you have two jugs or carboys, it would be much better to siphon directly into one of these pre-cleaned and sanitized containers than to use the open fermenter at this stage. This way, less wine is exposed to the air during racking. When siphoning, the mouth of the siphon tube should be kept as near the bottom of the receiving container as possible, so you will not create any splash, as even splashing the wine will expose it to oxygen.

As we have also mentioned, too much wine surface exposed to air, even in a sealed jug or carboy can cause oxidation. Therefore, keep the jug or carboy filled close to the neck; and use the proper size jug or carboy for each batch.

FLOWERS OF WINE

Completely fermented wine may be contaminated with "flowers of wine." Flowers of wine usually appear in containers that are not kept full, with too much surface exposed to oxygen. They start out as white beads on the surface, and if not treated, will eventually spread over the entire surface. If this happens, it is too late to correct the problem. What is taking place is that the flowers, which are a bacterial growth, are working in the opposite direction of fermentation. That is the flowers live on alcohol and oxygen, converting these to carbon dioxide and water. What will emerge is a lifeless, tasteless drink that is no good at all. Luckily the problem can be eliminated easily if discovered early enough. At the first sign of flowers, strain your wine through a tight woven piece of cloth, such as a piece of sanitized bed sheet. Then treat your wine with 1 campden tablet per gallon of wine and keep it topped off.

We suggest that you always use campden tablets when racking. A finished wine should contain trace amounts of SO2. Experts recommend 30 to 60 parts per million, a level that should be maintained throughout the process, right up to the time the finished bottle is opened. This is why a freshly opened bottle of wine is allowed to breathe for about 30 minutes before the wine is consumed. That time lapse gives the SO2 time to leave, so that it will not be detected by your tastebuds.

HYDROMETER
AND HOW TO USE

Hydrometers are instruments of measure used in various fields of activity. A 3 scale hydrometer used in winemaking is very useful, and it can serve at least three purposes. You can tell how much sugar to add to the must by determining how much natural sugar the juice of the fruit you use contains. You are able to determine more accurately whether you are making a dry or sweet wine. You can even get a measurement that will give you a good estimate of the potential alcohol content of your wine. You can also determine if your wine is completely worked out or stuck, by using a hydrometer.

We said a hydrometer is useful! Perhaps we should revise that statement and say, "a hydrometer is essential". You can make wine without one, just as you can make candy without a thermometer. However, if you do use one, you will end up knowing a lot more about what you are doing when making your wine.

One problem a few people have, though, is understanding how to use the hydrometer. They are intimidated by the charts and figures, and tend to shy away from using them, so the instrument sometimes simply gathers dust on the back of the shelf. Therefore, we have tried to make this section easy to understand, and hope that it will help you decide to use the hydrometer you already have, or to buy one and use it.

We suggest that you buy a 3 scale hydrometer, a plastic hydrometer sample jar, and a plastic wine thief, or the type of baster you use in the kitchen for gravy, etc. (For removing the wine from its container to put into the sample jar.) One scale will be Brix-balling, the second Potential Alcohol, and the third Specific Gravity or SG. Since different books on wine making refer to different scales, the 3 scale hydrometer should suffice.

HOW TO USE

Let's start out by taking a reading from the juice of the fruit you are going to make wine from, before adding anything to the juice. Remember this, when you take a reading from the hydrometer when it is floating in the must, the pulp, sugar or any other additives in the mixture will affect the reading by making the instrument float higher. Since you are now trying to determine how much natural sugar the juice contains, you should strain out all the pulp you can beforehand.

Water has an SG of 1.000. If the reading on the hydrometer is 1.025 we are showing here that your must is .025 heavier than plain water. From this you can tell how much material nature (or later, you) has added to water. If you were to take water and add it to some 180 proof alcohol, the hydrometer will show an SG below 1.000 because the alcohol is lighter than water. This is why we often can get a reading in a dry wine of below 1.000. There is enough alcohol in dry wine to let the hydrometer sink below the 1.000 mark.

If for some reason, you need to know the exact percentage, it is possible to measure the alcohol content of finished wines with an ebulliometer. It is a very accurate and expensive instrument, costing upwards of several hundred dollars.

ADJUSTING THE SUGAR AND PROBABLE ALCOHOL CONTENT OF WINE

Let's go through the steps on using a hydrometer when making wine. The ideal percentage of alcohol for a dry table wine is between 11% and 13%, as it is a wine we consume with food during meals.

We begin with the juice, plus water if needed, to dilute the acid content. Nothing else--sugar, acids, tannin-- nothing has been added to the juice at this stage, with the possible exception of water. Clean, sanitize and rinse well, your hydrometer, sample jar and wine thief. Using a wine thief or baster, extract the amount of must needed to float the hydrometer in the sample jar. Insert the hydrometer into the sample jar big end down, giving the hydrometer a slight spin as you do so. The spin releases any air bubbles that may be attached to the hydrometer which could throw your reading off a little. You will probably get a reading of around 1.025, give or take ten points because of the considerable variation of natural sugar in fruits.

Now we add about three to six cups of sugar water syrup per gallon to the must, mixing it in well. Take another sample and place it in the clean sample jar. Hopefully you will have a reading of 1.090 specific gravity (SG), if not, add more sugar syrup, a small amount at a time, to bring the reading up to 1.090 --1.095. When the reading reaches this measurement, the must has the correct amount of sugar to make a dry wine with a probable alcohol content of 11%.

Here is how to see this with the three scale hydrometers: remove the hydrometer from the sample jar and hold it in your right hand. Place your thumbnail on the 1.090 mark on the SG scale. Now, using your thumbnail to hold your place, begin to rotate the hydrometer to the right, or counterclockwise. The next scale to appear will be the potential alcohol scale. Stop at this scale and your thumbnail should be resting on the 11% potential alcohol. Notice the word "potential". This means, that if the yeast consumes all the sugar present in your wine, it will have an 11% alcohol content, and the final hydrometer reading with your finished wine would be 0% or 1.000. Continue rotating the hydrometer with your thumbnail still marking your place, and you should arrive at the Brix or Balling scale with a reading of 22 Brix. Now you know what to do when you read a recipe that calls for so many Brix of sugar. Some concentrates show a Brix reading on their labels. Using your three-scale hydrometer, you will be able to see what the potential alcohol of your wine will be. Of course, if you add sugar, you will need to take more readings.

Frustration is not desirable, so, for your own good, and to help you in making a better wine, don't get into the habit of making wine without a hydrometer. It really is one of the most important tools a winemaker can use. Among the other things we have mentioned, a hydrometer can also help you know when to bottle, and this will reduce the chance of renewed fermentation in the bottle, which can cause them to explode.

MAKING SWEET WINE

Let's say you are making a sweet wine using the three-scale hydrometer. Sweet wines generally have a higher alcohol content than dry wines. Some dessert wines go as high as 18%, and some that are fortified with alcohol go to 20%. Usually, it is possible for the home winemaker to reach 17% or 18% alcohol by using the right yeast and adding sugar to the wine in several stages rather than all at once.

Now to begin. Bring the must up to a reading of 1.120 SG by adding sugar syrup, two or three cups per gallon at a time, as you would with dry wine. Figure that the pulp in the must is causing a "misreading"of ten points, so that your true reading is 1.110, which corresponds to a potential alcohol reading of 14%. Now, if we were to work all the sugar out, down to an SG of 1.000, we would have an alcohol content of 14 1/2%. But we want a sweet wine with 17% alcohol! Each additional pound of sugar that we add will raise the alcohol percentage 5%. So working with a 14% must, we add one pound of sugar to get 17%. This should be added after most or all of the sugar added to the original must is worked out. Check the wine with your hydrometer frequently. When it gets down to 1.010 SG, add the pound of sugar syrup. Then work this out until the hydrometer shows a reading of 1.010 again.

At this point you have nearly reached the desired alcohol percentage. You are getting to the point where the wine is getting sweeter, not stronger. This is because when the wine approaches 17% or 18% alcohol the wine yeast generally dies. The alcohol is now too strong to support yeast life. The yeast dies and the remaining sugar is what will give the wine its sweet taste. When you think about it, if all the sugar in a batch were always worked out, you would always have a dry wine. This solves the mystery of why we said to add enough sugar to seemingly give 19%, when we only wanted 17%.

Let's suppose that you do not want to make a sweet wine with a high alcohol content. You can solve this by adding sugar or an artificial sweetener to the finished wine. <u>There is a danger of adding sugar to a finished wine, however</u>. The remaining yeast in the wine could start the fermentation again after you bottle and blow up the bottles. To prevent this from happening, you must either add an ingredient that will prevent further fermentation, or use a sweetening agent that will not ferment.

If your wine is worked out (finished), but you want it sweeter and you want to use a fermentable sugar, then add 1/2 teaspoon of SORBISTAT-K (potassium sorbate) per gallon of wine, and follow the instructions for use that come with it. Stir in the stabilizer and let the wine sit for two days. Then add the desired amount of sugar. Sorbistat-K, or potassium sorbate does not stop existing fermentation, but it will prevent a new fermentation from starting.

If you want to sweeten your wine without a fermentable sugar, you can try either lactose or any of the artificial sweeteners that are available today. Add only a little at a time, until you reach the level of sweetness you desire.

HYDROMETER

AIRLOCKS AND ADAPTERS

Airlocks and adapters are necessary in the secondary stage of fermentation. They are used to allow carbon dioxide to escape from your jug or carboy. At the same time, airlocks stop air from entering the jug or carboy. There are several types of airlocks and adapters available and they all follow the same principal, allowing gas to escape, and keeping air from entering. You just have to choose which one you prefer. If necessary you can even devise your own.

The home made type consists of a bored rubber stopper with a 1/4 or 3/8 inch clear soft plastic tubing, about 5 feet long. One end is inserted into the stopper that is placed in the mouth of your jug or carboy. The other end is placed in a container below the level of your wine fermenter. This container should be about half full of water or SO_2 solution. Make sure the end of the tube stays in the solution. One word of caution on this type airlock: If the temperature drops suddenly, and you have any air space in your fermenter, a vacuum could be created, drawing the liquid from the receiving container up through the tubing and into your fermenter. If this should happen, the liquid could contaminate your wine.

Three-piece plastic airlock. The stem of the airlock fits into a bored rubber stopper which fits into the mouth of the jug or carboy. It also fits into a rubber hood adapter which fits over the outside of the neck of the jug or carboy. This airlock has a check valve, and when the airlock is about half filled with water or SO2 solution, the check valve prevents air from backing into the fermenter. It also has a dust cap for the top. As the gas escapes through the lock, the check valve works up and down, indicating you have active fermentation. This action will slow down and stop when fermentation ceases. We prefer this type, as after it is used, it can be taken apart, cleaned and made ready for another fermentation.

Another type is the "S" shaped airlock. This airlock is also made of plastic and is a one piece airlock with a dust cap. The stem of this airlock also fits into a bored rubber stopper or a rubber hood adapter. Half way up the stem an "S" is formed. There is a bubble on both arms. When filled with water or SO2 solution, the bubbles act as the valve. You can watch the gas bubbles escape through the liquid. When fermentation is complete, the liquid in the bubble will be at the same level. You will not see any gas bubbles.

Airlock adapters allow you to use the same

airlock for different size jugs, or carboys. Generally they come in sizes for one gallon jugs and three, five and six gallon carboys, as these are the most common sizes used. They are available however, in almost any size you might need.

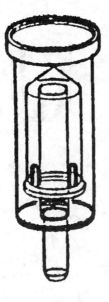

3 - Piece
Airlock

Adaptor

BASIC WINEMAKING EQUIPMENT

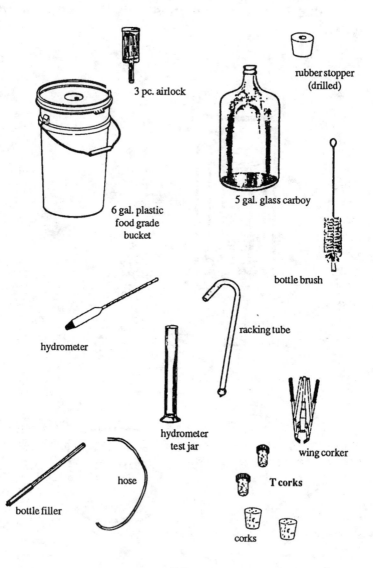

3 pc. airlock

rubber stopper
(drilled)

6 gal. plastic
food grade
bucket

5 gal. glass carboy

bottle brush

hydrometer

racking tube

hydrometer
test jar

wing corker

hose

T corks

bottle filler

corks

68

WINEMAKING EQUIPMENT

The winemaking equipment we recommend (with the exception of the corks) can be used over and over, every time you make wine. Which, if you enjoy making wine as much as we do, we hope is often.

If you plan on making one to three gallons of wine, from the recipes in this book, you may not want to go to the expense (although they only cost a few dollars) of buying and acid test kit, and a sulfite test kit. If you follow the recipes and instructions closely and use a hydrometer, your endeavor can produce a good wine.

However, due to the effort and time expended when making five or more gallons of wine, we strongly suggest that you buy an acid test kit and a sulfite test kit. As the more wine you make, the more critical the proper amounts of acid and sulfite in your wine becomes, in order to produce a good wine.

You may have some of the equipment on hand, and the rest of it can be purchased at a home wine and beermaking supply store.

ONE GALLON WINE EQUIPMENT

1 - Bucket - 3 gallon, food grade plastic

2 - Gallon jugs, glass

1 - Airlock

1 - Airlock adapter, (drilled rubber stopper) that will fit a gallon jug

1 - Racking tube - for siphoning wine from one container to another

1 - Siphon tubing - 3/8 inch x 5 feet with shut off clamp - attach to racking tube

1 - Bottle filler - with shut off valve

1 - Bottle brush - clean bottles and gallon jugs

1 - Hydrometer - 3 scale - specific gravity, Brix, potential alcohol - and a hydrometer test jar

1 - Thermometer - floating preferable, but others can be used

1 - Quart size fruit jar - with non metal or coated lid, for mixing sanitizing solution

Sanitizer- B-T-F iodine, potassium metabisulfite or sodium bisulfite.

Cleaner - Chlorinated T S P (tri sodium phosphate) - for cleaning equipment (soap and detergents are not recommended)

1 - Large pan (not aluminum) or food grade plastic bucket - 10 to 12 quart, for crushing fruit, etc.

1 - Spoon - about 20 inches long, stainless steel or plastic, for stirring crushed fruit and/ or juice

1 - Nylon filter bag - for crushing and pressing fruit, etc.

1 - 36 x 36 inch soft clear plastic sheet to cover primary container, tie to top of container

1 - Funnel - that will fit in neck of one gallon jug

1 - Tool - like potato masher, for crushing fruit, etc.

5 - Wine bottles - 750 ml size, or 10, 375 ml size and corks. The size is usually imprinted on the bottom rim of the bottle

5 or10 - Wine corks - standard wine corks, size 9 x 1 3/4"

1 - Corker - wing style, if you use standard wine corks,

Or if you use T corks
5 or10 - T corks, no corker needed

FIVE GALLON WINE EQUIPMENT

The following equipment is recommended for making a five gallon batch of wine. As you will see, there is not much difference between the equipment needed for making one gallon and five gallons of homemade wine. If you want to make a larger quantity of wine, all you will need is another 10 gallon or larger primary fermenter, more five gallon carboys, airlocks and airlock adapters, and of course more wine bottles.

1 -10 Gallon, food grade primary fermenter

1 - 5 gallon carboy, glass bottles

1 - Airlock

1 - Airlock adapter

1 - Racking tube

1 - Siphon hose, 5 ft. x 3/8 inch

1 - Bottle filler, with shut off valve

1 - Bottle brush

1 - Carboy brush

1 - Hydrometer, Three scale

1 - Thermometer, floating type preferred

1 - Gallon jug, for sanitizing solution

Sanitizer- B-T-F iodine, potassium metabisulfite or sodium bisulfite

Cleaner - Chlorinated T S P (tri sodium phosphate)

1 - Spoon - about 20" long, stainless steel or plastic for stirring

1 - Large pan (not aluminum) or plastic bucket,

10 to 20 quart, for crushing fruit, etc.

1 - Nylon filter bag, (large) for crushing and pressing fruit, etc.

1 - Tool - for crushing fruit, etc. Or a

Grape crusher or crusher stemmer, and a

Grape or fruit press

1 - 36 x 36 inch soft clear plastic sheet

1 - Funnel - that will fit the neck of a carboy

25 - Wine bottles, 750 ml size

25 - Wine corks, size 9 x 1 3/4"

1 - Wing style hand corker

1 - Acid Test Kit

73

1 - Titret Test Kit (for testing sulfites)

You can usually buy a complete winemaking equipment kit, for less money than if you buy single items, at a home wine and beermaking supply store.

A five gallon batch of wine, usually takes about 80 lbs. of grapes. You can usually rent, or you can buy a grape press, a crusher, or a crusher / stemmer from your local home wine supply store.

SANITIZING

Washing, rinsing and sanitizing all equipment used is very important. We believe this is the most crucial single procedure in making wine.

SANITIZING EQUIPMENT

Wash all your equipment in lukewarm chlorinated Tri Sodium Phosphate (TSP). 1/4 cup of TSP to one gallon of warm water will make a strong sanitizing solution. Rinse to make sure you have removed all traces of the TSP. If you are sure your equipment is clean and you are going to use it immediately, it probably does not need any further sanitizing. If you are not going to start your wine until the next day or later, you should sanitize your equipment again at that time.

For the purpose of sanitizing, you can use a product called B-T-F Iodine sanitizer. It comes in a liquid form that makes it extremely convenient to use, and the color when mixed

75

with water makes it easy to judge quantities to use. If you can see any color, you've probably added enough. The recommended usage of 12 ppm (parts per million) is the level used in many breweries without a subsequent rinse. This is helpful especially if you believe your local water to be a source of bacteria, and if rinsing in such water would be likely to re-inoculate harmful matter to your equipment. If your water quality is not a problem, a rinse can be helpful, and reassuring, just in case you've been a bit heavy-handed with the sanitizer as we tend to be.

You can also use potassium metabisulfite or sodium bisulfite powder as a sanitizer. Dissolve about 4 oz. of potassium metabisulphite, or sodium bisulfite in a gallon of water and rinse your equipment with it. Then rinse all equipment with clean water except bottles. You can let them drain and dry, in an upside down position.

If the sanitizers mentioned cannot be obtained, a sanitizer can be made with regular, unscented household bleach. Use one (1) ounce of bleach, mixed in 2 and 1/2 gallons of water. Rinse all the equipment you are going to use with the solution. Then rinse with clean water again, and again, until you are positive you have removed all traces of the bleach.

90 "To the health of the grape" (Honoré Daumier)

4   The Grapevine (Aristide Maillol)

MAKING ONE TO FIVE GALLONS OF WINE

Many recipes for homemade wine are written for one gallon quantities. Personally, we prefer to make wine in a 3 or 5 gallon quantity so that we have a good sized batch when we are done. A gallon of homemade wine will produce about five 750 ml bottles of wine. While with a five gallon batch of wine, you can count on about twenty-five 750 ml bottles. This amount means that you will not only have enough for you and your family, but you will also have some you can share with your friends, if you so choose.

If you are uncertain whether you would care for the taste of a certain wine, be it from the grape or a fruit, but you would still like to try it, then go ahead and make a gallon of the wine. If you find that you do like it, you can always make a larger batch. If you find you do not care for it, you didn't make enough to worry about. Experimenting with gallon test batches is very interesting and you can learn quite a bit about winemaking while making them.

For the beginner, home winemaking is often more convenient for them when working with smaller batches, but it is also fairly easy for them to make a larger batch of wine. We have included a number of recipes for one, three and five gallons. For any one gallon recipe, you can, except for the yeast, usually multiply the ingredients and come up with a larger batch. Let's say you want to make five gallons of wine with a one gallon recipe. Just multiply all the ingredients by five, except the yeast. One package of wine yeast, made into a starter, will make one to five gallons of wine.

It does not make any difference whether you are making one gallon of wine, five gallons of wine or more. The basic processes are always the same regardless of the size of the batch of wine.

WINEMAKING WITH CONCENTRATES

There are several good reasons for making wine with red or white <u>grape or fruit concentrates</u>. First you should probably know a little about them. Very complex and elaborate machinery is used by a processor to prepare a <u>grape concentrate</u>. Grape concentrate is not a can or bottle of grape juice. It is the juice of grapes reduced in volume by as much as four or five times. The concentration of juices means that you will be able to make five gallons of a full bodied red or white wine, 12% alcohol, with three 46 oz. cans of concentrate.

One reason for using concentrates is, believe it or not, economy. Unless you or a generous friend live in an orchard or vineyard, you undoubtedly will have to pay for the fruit that is available. As for fruit that is not available, or out of season, money can't buy it because you can't get it unless you already froze it or had it trucked in.

This brings us to another reason, actually a two part reason; seasonal and geographical.

Let's say you live in Montana and you want to make a Zinfandel wine in January. Say you live in a section of the country where no grapes will grow and you would like to make your own Pinot Chardonnay. Then concentrates are the way to go. The great idea about concentrates is that you can make wine year round from many fruits, berries or grapes that usually are not available to you most or all of the time.

Some fruits, such as apples, pears, peaches, and even cherries are somewhat difficult to prepare in the process of getting them ready for making wine. Often the home winemaker will find the job of paring, coring and cutting the fruit into small pieces more than they bargained for and wish they had not started the whole thing. For those who have tried this method and found it too much trouble, and would still like to make their own fruit wine the easy way, fruit base concentrates are the solution. They are also available all year long so you can make wine any time you want to.

Fruit base concentrates are not just a can of fruit. They are solid pack fruit in their own natural juice, and they are processed the same way as grape concentrates.

The differences between grape concentrate (which is all juice and does not contain any grapes to crush and press) and fruit base concentrates, is that you do need to crush and press the fruit. However, and a blessing, all the other work has been done for you, such as picking, sorting good from bad fruit, coring, paring and cutting into small pieces.

There are European, as well as American concentrates. Imported concentrate, just like some imported wines, are often of good quality, but so are those made in the United States. After trying several concentrates made in the United States you might want to try one from Europe for comparison.

Always read the label on a can of concentrate, and follow the printed instructions.

Just to show you how easy it is to make wine from grape concentrate, we will give you some suggested instructions.

Clean and sanitize your equipment, in an SO2 solution, rinse and drain.

Open the can or cans of concentrate and pour into a primary container. (The primary container should be at least one or two gallons larger than the amount of wine you are going to make.) Rinse the cans in warm water to remove any concentrate that is left in them. Then add the rest of the cold water that is needed for the recipe.

Stir in the amount of sugar needed for the recipe, and (except for the wine yeast, which you will add later) stir in all the other ingredients. Stirring will help the ingredients dissolve.

Cover the container with a piece of clear plastic sheet and tie it to the top of the container. Using clear plastic, lets you look into in the container. Allow it to sit overnight in a room temperature of about 70 degrees F.

Make a yeast starter, such as we suggest on page 93   and let it sit overnight along with the container of must.

Pour the yeast starter into the must and stir. Cover the container of must with the clear plastic. Again, with clear plastic, you can watch the fermentation which should start in a few hours to a day.

Fermentation will be vigorous. When it slows down, use a racking tube and siphon the wine into a clean, sanitized jug or carboy. When you siphon, try your best not to disturb the sediment on the bottom of the container. If the amount of juice you have is going to overflow the receiving container, save it. Keep it in the refrigerator, and if needed, use it later to top off your wine as the fermentation slows to a crawl. Always leave a couple of inches or more of air space between the airlock and the top of the wine. The amount of air space depends on how vigorous the fermentation is. Your wine is now in a secondary fermenter.

Attach an airlock to the jug or carboy. Make sure you fill the airlock half way with an SO2 solution or water.

In 10 to 14 days rack (siphon) into another clean sanitized jug or carboy; as most of the sediment in the wine should have settled to the bottom by now. If needed, add a little water or sugar syrup to top off.

Rack again in two months. If the wine is not clear, wait another month and rack it again.

(See bottling instructions we have included in the book on page 98 and 99)

Finally, if we seem up on the subject of concentrates, there are good reasons for it. We have made wine from both fresh fruit and grapes. They were all good, but look at the advantages of concentrates: easy to prepare, available year round and in some varieties sometimes not available to you any other way.

Many Concentrates contain SO$_2$ as a preservative

To be on the safe side, add all ingredients except the yeast.

Let stand overnight, covered.
Next day add the yeast.

GRAPE CONCENTRATES

Chenin Blanc
Emerald Riesling
French Colombard
Gewurztraminer
Grey Riesling
Johannisberg Riesling
Liebfraumilch
Muscat
Pinot Chardonnay
Premium Chabli
Sauvignon Blanc
Semillon
Symphony
Vino Blanc
Grenache Rose
Rose
Barbera
Cabernet
Cabernet Sauvignon
Gamay Beaujolais
Merlot
Petite Sirah
Pinot Noir
Premium Burgundy
Ruby Cabernet
Vino Rosso (Red)
Zinfandel
Zinfandel Blush

One 46 ounce can will make 5 gallons of light bodied wine with 8% alcohol. Two cans will make 5 gallons of medium bodied wine with 10% alcohol. Three cans will make 5 gallons of full bodied wine with 12% alcohol.

Five gallons of wine and the percentage of alcohol are approximately what you will end up with; allowing for spillage and/ or the amount of sugar and water you add. Follow the recipe that comes with the concentrate.

FRUIT WINE BASES

Apple Concentrate

Apricot Wine Base

Blackberry Wine Base

Blueberry Wine Base

Boysenberry Wine Base

Cherry Wine Base

Cranberry Wine Base

Elderberry Wine Base

Gooseberry Wine Base

Loganberry Wine Base

Marionberry Wine Base

Peach Wine Base

Plum Wine Base

Raspberry Wine Base

Strawberry Wine Base

Fruit wine base is packed in 96 oz. cans and comes with a recipe for 5 gallons of wine.

GENERAL STEPS

1. crush the fruit

2. add all ingredients except the yeast let stand over night

cover to keep bugs, etc. out

3. next day....
add the yeast starter & stir

LET STAND OVERNIGHT AGAIN, COVERED

4. 3rd day start stirring twice a day

SOMETIMES "MUST" OVERFLOWS SO BE PREPARED

5. after about 5 - 7 days

strain pulp out

pour juice into carboy

attach airlock

After about 3 to 4 weeks....

Rack every 3 months
or so
till it is done;

then let it sit another month or so to make sure it's done!

Finally, bottle

first, soak corks in
sodium bisulfite solution
for 20 minutes...

voilá

METHODOLOGY FOR WINEMAKING

The following basic procedure may be used for all the recipes in this book. However, read the instructions for each recipe, as there will be variations in the preparation of some fruit and vegetables.

When using a hydrometer, the starting specific gravity reading for most of the recipes should be between 1.090 and 1.100. If the reading is not this high, add some more sugar water, a little at a time, to bring the reading up.

The approximate desirable acid level for red grape wine is .65% to .75%. White grape wine .70% to .80%. Fruit wines .60%.

Sort through the berries, fruit, grapes or vegetables the recipe calls for and remove all the leaves, stems, any that are green or moldy, and any other foreign material. Use only good sound produce.

For small batches, crush the berries or fruit into a pulp, in a pan, or chop the fruit or

91

vegetables as directed.   When you get them crushed and/ or chopped, transfer the pulp and juice to the food grade plastic container (primary fermenter).

If you are going to make a large batch of wine and plan to use a fruit or grape press, some fruit, such as apples and pears need to be chopped before pressing. Apricots, cherries, peaches and plums should be de-stoned.

While you are crushing or chopping, you can dissolve the amount of sugar the recipe calls for, pour it into a large pan, cover with water, stir, and heat until hot, stirring occasionally. Allow to cool to 80 - 85 degrees F.

PRIMARY FERMENTATION

Pour the warm sugar water over the prepared berries, fruit or vegetables in the fermenter and stir.   Then add the rest of the water. (Use a total of one gallon of water for a one gallon batch, three gallons for a three gallon batch or a total of five gallons of water for a five gallon batch.) Along with the ingredients this may seem like more liquid than is needed, but remember you will lose some when you rack the wine off the sediment.

Now, crush the campden tablet(s), dissolve in a little water, and add all the ingredients the recipe calls for, except for the yeast.   (The wine yeast will be added later.)

Cover the fermenter with a clear plastic sheet and <u>let the must in the fermenter sit over night</u> in a warm area around 70 degrees F. This amount of time allows the campden tablet (SO2) enough time to destroy any wild yeast and other bacteria in the crushed berries, fruit or grapes and juice.

By now, enough SO2 has escaped so that what remains will not destroy your yeast. You should now start a yeast starter.

YEAST STARTER

Using a sanitized cup, take about 1/2 to 1 cup of juice from the must in the fermenter. Pour it into a sanitized pint jar or large glass and add the same amount of boiled cool water. Open the packet and add the wine yeast. Stir to dissolve any lumps and let this sit covered for a few hours. One packet of dry yeast contains many thousands of yeast cells. When made into a starter, these thousands of yeast cells multiply into thousands more. This is why we use a starter; it jump starts your yeast and gives it a much better chance of starting a strong fermentation.

After the yeast starter has set for a few hours, pour it into the must in the primary fermenter and stir.

Keep the fermenting must in a warm area, around 70 degrees F., and the fermentation should become active within a few hours. At this point, primary fermentation has begun.

93

Stir the must every day for about five to six days, or until when you check it with your hydrometer, the specific gravity reading is 1.040.

SUMMARY OF STEPS
PRIMARY FERMENTATION STAGE

1---Assemble ingredients and equipment

2---Prepare sanitizing solution and sanitize equipment

3---Prepare fruit and add to primary fermenter

4---Heat water in a pan, pour in sugar and stir until dissolved, cool and pour into fermenter and stir

5---Add all other ingredients (except yeast) to fermenter include crushed and dissolved campden tablet(s), stir

6---Let it sit overnight

7---Prepare yeast starter, let it sit for a few hours

8---Now add yeast starter to the must

9---Stir the must daily

SECONDARY FERMENTATION

You are now ready to move on to the second stage of fermentation. The first thing you do is assemble the equipment you will need and sanitize it.

First, rinse the airlock, the adapter and the glass jug or carboy with water. (Hopefully, they were washed the week before. If not, wash them.) Then sanitize them with the sanitizing solution. Pour some of the solution into the jug or carboy and shake well to sanitize the inside of the container.

If using juice fermentation, siphon (rack) the juice from the primary fermenter into a jug or carboy (secondary fermenter). Try not to disturb the sediment in the bottom of the primary container. Siphon only the juice.

If using pulp fermentation, press and strain into secondary jugs. Allow room for a small amount of temporary foaming in the secondary jugs. When foaming subsides, top up with water or extra wine. Now, insert the airlock and its adapter into the mouth of the jug or carboy, making sure the adapter is in tight. Remove the dust cover from the airlock, fill the airlock about half full with SO2 solution (potassium metabisulfite). Be careful not to pour the solution down the hole into your wine. Your wine has just now entered its secondary fermentation stage.

The gases from the fermentation process

will be escaping through the airlock, which will cause a bubbling action in the liquid in the airlock. The wine should be left to stand now for about three to four weeks. At that time you will prepare to rack the wine.

Racking is the process of removing the wine off the sediment (lees) that collects on the bottom of the fermenter. To rack, you will need another jug or carboy and the racking tube and siphon tubing. Wash and sanitize the container, racking tube and tubing just as you did for the first (primary) stage. Place the jug or carboy containing the fermenting wine in a position above the empty container, jug or carboy. Remove the airlock and adapter, and insert the racking tube deep into the wine, siphon (rack) off the wine above the sediment. Be careful not to disturb the sediment, and leave as much of it as possible on the bottom of the container. Discard the sediment. Wash and sanitize the airlock and adapter, and the empty jug or carboy you just siphoned from. At this time add one dissolved campden tablet for each gallon of wine. Make sure the carboys or jugs are filled within 2" of the top.   Attach the airlock and adapter, and half fill the airlock with SO2.

In another four to six weeks, the fermentation should be very slow. You will be able to detect very little activity in the airlock. It is time to rack again. Repeat the process as before. After racking remember to keep the jug or carboy filled within 2" of the top.

In about four weeks, rack again. By now the wine should be clearing thoroughly. Let it sit another three or four weeks. By now, all the fermentation should be worked completely out. Your wine should be ready for bottling. Although most wine will clear itself, if you feel it is not clear enough, check the portion of this book that discusses methods for clarifying wine.

SUMMARY SECONDARY STAGE

1---Sanitize equipment

2---Press or strain must into jug or carboy

3---Top off carboys and attach airlocks

4---Rack wine, rack wine, rack wine

5---Sanitize bottles and corks

6---Bottle the wine

<u>Bottling Time</u>

Fermentation has stopped. The wine is clear. It is time to bottle. We suggest the use of corkers and standard corks. For the beginner who may only want to make one small batch of wine, it is an expense you might want to forego until you have the inclination to make a few more batches. We have set out a method for bottling that does not require a corker, but for details on using a corker check the section under corks and corkers.

The first step in bottling is to wash the bottles. Rinse thoroughly and then sanitize all the bottles and corks. If you do not have a corker, wine bottles will accept "T" corks. A "T" cork looks like the letter T, by the way, and inserts into the bottle easily. Your home wine supply store will probably have them in stock.

On to actual bottling. At bottling time it is always a good idea to add a stabilizer such as Sorbistat K (Potassium sorbate) to your wine. A stabilizer will not stop present active fermentation, but it will prevent renewed fermentation.

Just as in racking, you will place the wine in the jug or carboy on a level higher than the receiving bottles. Using a siphon tubing and a bottle filler with a shut off valve, push the bottle filler down on the bottom of the bottle and the wine will start to flow. When it reaches the top of the bottle, release the pressure on the bottle filler and the wine will stop flowing. Remove the bottle filler from the bottle and you will have the proper amount of air space in the top of the bottle.

If you are going to use "T" corks, the bottles should be stored upright rather than on their sides. If you use a corker and standard corks, the bottles should stand upright at least five days after bottling to allow pressure to escape from the bottles. Then store them on their sides or upside down to keep the corks from drying out and shrinking, which can cause the wine to leak.

If you have carefully followed all these steps, your wine should be of good quality. A dry wine should age for at least a year. Fruit wines are usually quite drinkable in six months, but better in nine to twelve months.

37   Wine Coopers (Thomas Rowlandson)

WINE RECIPES

BERRY, FRUIT & VEGETABLE

All the recipes in the book are meant as guide lines only. Adjustments may be necessary for various recipes, according to the growing conditions for the berry, fruit or vegetable. When using a hydrometer, (please do) the starting Specific Gravity for each recipe should be about 1.090 to 1.095. The Acid content about .60% to .65%.

BLACKBERRY, BOYSENBERRY, LOGANBERRY, MARIONBERRY OR SALALBERRY

ONE GALLON

4 pounds ripe berries
2 and 1/2 pounds cane sugar
1 teaspoon powdered yeast nutrient

1 teaspoon acid blend
1 campden tablet, crush and dissolve
1 package all purpose wine yeast
1 gallon water

FIVE GALLONS

20 pounds ripe berries
12 and 1/2 pounds cane sugar
5 teaspoons powdered yeast nutrient
5 teaspoons acid blend
5 campden tablets, crush and dissolve
1 package all purpose wine yeast
5 gallons water

Use only fully ripe berries. Sort through them carefully to be sure none are moldy. Remove leaves, stems and rinse the berries in cold water, drain well.

Methodology: refer to page 91 through 98.

APPLE WINE

ONE GALLON

8 pounds apples
1 teaspoon acid blend
1 teaspoon yeast nutrient powder
1/2 teaspoon pectic enzyme
2 and 1/2 pounds cane sugar
1/4 teaspoon grape tannin
1 campden tablet, crush and dissolve
1 package all purpose or Cote des Blancs
  wine yeast
1 gallon water

THREE GALLONS

Multiply all the ingredient by 3, except the yeast, one package will make 1 to 5 gallons of wine.

FIVE GALLONS

40 pounds apples
5 teaspoons acid blend
5 teaspoon yeast nutrient powder
2 and 1/2 teaspoons pectic enzyme
12 and 1/2 pounds cane sugar
1 and 1/4 teaspoon grape tannin
5 campden tablets, crush and dissolve
1 package all purpose or Cote des Blancs
  wine yeast
5 gallons water

A mixture of cooking, delicious, and crab

103

apples make a very good wine.

For one gallon batch, cut apples in small pieces, core and mince. For five gallon batch, do the same, or cut in small pieces and press in a grape or apple press.

Methodology: see page 91 through 98.

APRICOT-CHERRY-PEACH or PLUM WINE

ONE GALLON

3 pounds fresh fruit
Or 2 pounds sour cherries, if you make
 sour cherry wine
2 and 1/2 pounds cane sugar
1 and 1/2 teaspoons acid blend
1/4 teaspoon grape tannin
1 and 1/4 teaspoons yeast nutrient
 powder
1/2 teaspoon pectic enzyme
1 campden tablet, crush and dissolve
1 package all purpose or LALVIN K1-V1116
 wine yeast
1 gallon water

THREE GALLONS

Multiply all the ingredients by 3, except
the yeast, one package of wine yeast will make 1
to 5 gallons of wine.

FIVE GALLONS

15 pounds fresh fruit
 or 10 pounds sour cherries, if you make
 sour cherry wine.
12 and 1/2 pounds cane sugar
7 and 1/2 teaspoons of acid blend
1 and 1/4   teaspoons grape tannin
6 and 1/4 teaspoons yeast nutrient
 powder
2 and 1/2 teaspoons pectic enzyme

5 campden tablets, crush and dissolve
1 package all purpose or
LALVIN K1-V1116 wine yeast
5 gallons water

Use ripe, good fruit. Cut out the bad spots and pit all the fruit. Then mash thoroughly.

Methodology: see page 91 through 98.

BANANA WINE

ONE GALLON

2 and 1/2 pounds ripe (not overripe)
 bananas
2 and 1/2 pounds cane sugar
1 pound raisins
1 teaspoon yeast nutrient powder
1/4 teaspoon grape tannin
3 teaspoons acid blend
1 campden tablet, crush and dissolve
1 package champagne yeast
1 gallon water

    Chop or mince raisins. Put the raisins
and sugar in a pan. Add 1/2 gallon of water
and bring to a boil.   Allow to cool. Mash
bananas and put the raisins and bananas in
primary fermenter. Add another 1/2 gallon of
water

    If you wish to make 5 gallons of banana
wine, multiply all the ingredients amount by 5,
except the amount of yeast. One package of
yeast will make 1 to 5 gallons of wine.

    Methodology: see page 91 through 98.

BEET WINE

ONE GALLON

3 pounds beets
2 and 1/2 pounds cane sugar
2 teaspoons acid blend
1 teaspoon yeast nutrient powder
1/4 teaspoon grape tannin
1 campden tablet, crush and dissolve
1 package all purpose wine yeast
1 gallon hot water

Discard leaves and any root. Wash and peel the beets. Cut into small pieces. Place in a nylon or muslin straining bag (fasten the top of the bag so the beet pieces don't fall out). Put the bag in a pan, add a gallon of water and simmer until the beet pieces are tender. Pour the sugar into the hot water, stir to dissolve. When cool, pour the juice into the fermenter. Also place the bag containing the beet pieces into the fermenter. Add all the other ingredients (except the yeast). Cover the fermenter with a clear plastic sheet and let sit overnight. The next day add the yeast starter. See yeast starter, page 93.

After about 5 or 6 days or when the specific gravity reading is about 1.040, remove and press the bag of beet pulp lightly to extract the juice and discard the pulp.

The wine is now ready for the second stage.   See secondary fermentation, page 95

<u>See secondary fermentation, page 95 through
page 98.</u>

If you want to make more than one gallon,
just multiply the amounts of all the ingredients
(except the yeast) by the number of gallons you
want to make. One package of yeast will make
one to five gallons of wine.

BLUEBERRY WINE

ONE GALLON

2 and 1/2 pounds ripe blueberries
2 and 1/4 pounds cane sugar
1 and 1/2 teaspoons acid blend
1/2 teaspoon pectic enzyme
1 teaspoon yeast nutrient powder
1 campden tablet, crush and dissolve
1 package all purpose wine yeast
1 gallon water

THREE GALLONS

Multiply all the ingredients by 3, except the yeast One package of yeast will make 1 to 5 gallons of wine.

FIVE GALLONS

12 and 1/2 pounds ripe blueberries
11 and 1/4 pounds cane sugar
7 and 1/2 teaspoons acid blend
2 and 1/2 teaspoons pectic enzyme
4 teaspoons yeast nutrient powder
5 campden tablets, crush and dissolve
1 package all purpose wine yeast
5 gallons water

Use only good, ripe berries. Sort through and remove stems, leaves, green and / or moldy berries. Wash the berries and drain well.

Methodology: see page 91 through 98.

110

CHOKECHERRY WINE

ONE GALLON

2 pounds chokecherries
1 and 1/2 pounds minced raisins
2 and 1/2 pounds cane sugar
1 teaspoon acid blend
1/2 teaspoon pectic enzyme
1 teaspoon yeast nutrient powder
1 campden tablet, crush and dissolve
1 package all purpose wine yeast
1 gallon water

Use good, fully ripe chokecherries. Rinse and drain well. When you crush or mash the cherries, do not to break the very bitter pits.

Methodology: see page 91 through 98.

CRANBERRY WINE

ONE GALLON

3 pounds fresh cranberries
1 and 1/2 pounds raisins
2 and 1/2 pounds cane sugar
1/2 teaspoon pectic enzyme
1 teaspoon yeast nutrient powder
1 campden tablet, crush and dissolve
1 package all purpose wine yeast
1 gallon water

3 GALLONS

Multiply all the ingredients by 3, except the yeast. One package of yeast will make 1 to 5 gallons of wine.

Use good, ripe cranberries. Sort and remove all but the ripe berries. Remove leaves and stems, etc. Crush the berries and mince the raisins.

Methodology: see page 91 through 98.

DANDELION WINE

ONE GALLON

7 cups dandelion petals
1 pound white raisins
2 pounds cane sugar
3 teaspoons acid blend
1/4 teaspoon grape tannin
1 teaspoon yeast nutrient powder
1 campden tablet, crush and dissolve
1 package all-purpose wine yeast
1 gallon hot water

THREE GALLONS

21 cups dandelion petals
3 pound white raisins
6 pounds cane sugar
9 teaspoons acid blend
3/4 teaspoon grape tannin
3 teaspoons yeast nutrient powder
3 campden tablets, crush and dissolve
1 package all-purpose wine yeast
1 gallon hot water. Add all ingredients
 except wine yeast, stir and allow to set
 overnight, then add
2 gallons water (room temperature)

Use only good bright yellow petals. Do not use any stems or green parts. Some fields are sprayed, avoid them. Rinse the petals and drain well. Mince the raisins.

Methodology: see page 91 through 98.

FIG WINE

ONE GALLON

4 pounds fresh figs
2 and 1/2 pounds cane sugar
3 teaspoons acid blend
1 teaspoon yeast nutrient powder
1 campden tablet, crush and dissolve
1 package all purpose wine yeast
1 gallon water

Use only good, ripe figs. Watch for mold. Discard leaves and stems. Rinse and drain figs well. Chop in small pieces. Place the chopped figs in a straining bag. Put the bag of chopped figs into the primary fermenter. Add water and stir.

THREE GALLONS

12 pounds fresh figs
7 and 1/2 pounds cane sugar
9 teaspoons acid blend
3 teaspoons yeast nutrient powder
3 campden tablets, crush and dissolve
1 package of all purpose wine yeast
3 gallons water

Follow directions for one gallon

Methodology: see page 91 through 98.

GOOSEBERRY WINE

ONE GALLON

3 pounds fresh gooseberries
2 and 1/2 pounds cane sugar
1/2 teaspoon acid blend
1 teaspoon yeast nutrient powder
1 teaspoon pectic enzyme
1/8 teaspoon grape tannin
1 campden tablet, crush and dissolve
1 package all-purpose wine yeast
1 gallon water

Rinse and sort all the good, ripe berries from the bad. Pick out the leaves and stems. Put the berries in a straining bag, tie securely. Put the bag of berries in a pan and crush. Place the bag of crushed berries into the primary fermenter, then pour the juice into the fermenter. Add warm water and crushed, dissolved campden tablet and let the mixture set for 12 to 14 hours. Then add rest of ingredients, including yeast starter (page 93) and ferment for 3 days. Siphon off juice. Gently press the bag and strain juice into primary fermenter, discard pulp. Pour or siphon juice back into fermenter and ferment as usual. (Methodology, see page 95 through 98).

THREE GALLONS

9 pounds fresh gooseberries
7 and 1/2 pounds cane sugar
1 and 1/2 teaspoons acid blend

3 teaspoons yeast nutrient powder
3 teaspoons pectic enzyme powder
3/8 teaspoon grape tannin
3 campden tablets, crush and dissolve
1 package all-purpose wine yeast
3 gallons water

Follow directions for one gallon.

Methodology: see page 95 through 98.

HUCKLEBERRY
AND OREGON "GRAPE" WINE

The Oregon "grape" is not a true grape.

You might want to try this recipe, but as the acid content and the sugar level in the berries, or "grape" vary a great deal, it would be helpful to use an acid test kit and a hydrometer. The specific gravity should be around 1.095 to 1.100 and the acid level near .65%.

ONE GALLON

2 and 1/2 pounds berries or "grapes"
1 pound raisins
2 and 1/2 pounds cane sugar, or add
 sugar until specific gravity is between
1.095 and 1.100
1 teaspoon acid blend, or acid level near
 .65%
1 teaspoon yeast nutrient powder
1/4 teaspoon grape tannin
1 package all purpose wine yeast
1 campden tablet, crush and dissolve
1 gallon of water

These berries and "grapes" seem to be best if picked late in the season. Sort through them. Pick out all the bad and moldy fruit.. Rinse, drain well. Place in a straining bag and crush.

Methodology: see page 91 through 98

117

GRAPE WINE
RED

As the sugar level, acid level and even the moisture content of grapes can vary greatly from season to season, it makes it difficult to write a standard recipe for grape wine. To know what is going on with your potential wine, you should use a hydrometer, which on the balling scale, will give you the sugar content of your must. The sugar content should be 22% to 24% to give you a 12% alcohol wine. It will also give you the specific gravity of the must, which should be 1.095. You should also use an acid test kit which will give you the percentage of acid in your must. It should be .65%. If the acid content is too low or too high, you can adjust it.

If you make wine with grapes grown in the northeast part of the United States or Canada, your wine will probably need adjusting, as the grapes grown there are usually low in sugar and high in acid.

ONE GALLON RED WINE

16 to 18 pounds of red grapes
Sugar: if sugar content is low, add sugar to bring the
specific gravity up to 1.095
Acid: if acid content is low, add acid blend to bring it   up to .65%
1 teaspoon yeast nutrient powder
1 campden tablet, crush and dissolve
1 package all purpose wine yeast

5 GALLONS, RED WINE

80 to 90 pounds of red grapes
Sugar: if sugar content is low, add sugar
to bring the specific gravity to 1.095
Acid: if acid content is low, add acid blend
to bring it up to .65%
5 teaspoon yeast nutrient powder
5 campden tablets, crush and dissolve
1 package all purpose wine yeast

Sort out the grapes. Remove any that are not ripe or are moldy. Remove stems, leaves and any unrelated matter. Crush the grapes into a 2 to 10 gallon primary fermenter. Do not fill over 3/4 full as the must expands and could bubble over the top.

Test for the acid and the sugar content. If you do not have an acid test kit, at least test the sugar content with your hydrometer, which you should have.

Add one crushed campden tablet per gallon to the must and stir until you are sure the must is well stirred.

Cover the fermenter with a clear plastic sheet, and allow the must to sit over night in a warm area (65 to 80 F.)

Now, use a sanitized cup, and take 1/2 cup of the grape juice from the fermenter. To this add 1/2 cup of boiled and cooled water. Pour both into a pint jar or large glass. Add your wine yeast, stir to dissolve any lumps, and let sit for a couple of hours. Then pour the yeast starter into the must in the fermenter and stir. Place the plastic cover back on the top of the fermenter and tie down.

Stir the must daily to keep the must mixed and to keep the cap wet that will form on the top. In five or six days when the fermentation has slowed down, or the reading on your hydrometer is about 1.005 rack the wine.

Secondary fermentation, see page 95 through 98.

GRAPE WINE
WHITE

As when making red wine with red grapes, the sugar level, acid level and moisture content of white grapes must be considered when making white wine. Use a hydrometer to determine the sugar content of the grape juice, which should be about 22% to give the finished wine about 12% alcohol. Use an acid test kit to determine the acid content of the juice and adjust the acid content to .70%.

Unlike red wine, the fermentation of white wine does not take place on the pulp or skins of the grape.

ONE GALLON WHITE WINE

16 to 18 pounds of white grapes
Sugar: if sugar content is low, add sugar to bring the specific gravity up to 1.095
Acid: if acid content is low, add acid blend to bring it up to .70%
1 teaspoon yeast nutrient powder
1 campden tablet, crush and dissolve in warm water
1 package all purpose wine yeast

Sort out the grapes, Remove any that are not ripe or are moldy. Remove stems, leaves and any other foreign matter.

When making white wine, the less you stir or agitate it the better. In other words, the less air it encounters the better, as air causes oxidation which in turn causes the wine to turn brown and can also give it an off taste.

5 GALLONS, WHITE WINE

80 to 90 pounds of white grapes
Sugar: if sugar content is low, add sugar to bring the specific gravity up to 1.095
Acid: if acid content is low, add acid blend to bring it up to .70%
5 teaspoon yeast nutrient powder
5 campden tablets, crush and dissolve in warm water
1 package all purpose wine yeast

Sort out the grapes, Remove any that are not ripe or are moldy. Remove stems, leaves and any other foreign matter.

Instructions: 1 or 5 gallons

Crush the grapes into a container and directly add the crushed and dissolved campden tablets and stir. Then press as much juice as possible out of the crushed grapes (either using a straining bag or a grape press) into another container.

Allow the juice to settle for at least 12 hours before you rack off the juice into a fermenter. Do not fill the fermenter (5 gallon glass carboy) (water bottle) over 3/4 full.

Check the acid level of the juice with an

acid test kit, and if low adjust the level to .70% with acid blend. If the acid level is too high, dilute the juice with boiled and cooled water.

Check the sugar content of the juice with a hydrometer and if low, adjust the specific gravity level to 1.090 - 1.095 by adding cane sugar.

Add the yeast starter (page 93) and yeast nutrient.

For best results, white wine should be fermented at 70 degrees F. or lower. When fermented at this temperature it usually takes a little longer for the fermentation to begin. If there is no sign of fermentation, such as bubbles on the top, in 3 or 4 days, perhaps the juice is too cold, if so, raise the temperature. If that does not work, add more yeast starter.

In a few days after fermentation begins, vigorous fermentation will subside, and when the specific gravity has fallen to around 1.015, rack (page 97) into a clean fermenter (glass carboy) top off, and attach an airlock. See airlocks (page 65).

In about three weeks the specific gravity should have dropped to about 1.000. At this time rack the must into a clean sanitized carboy; being careful to have the racking tube extended to the bottom of the receiving fermenter to avoid getting air in the wine by splashing. Rack very carefully so as not to disturb the sediment in the bottom of the primary fermenter. When you have finished racking, add one crushed and dissolved campden tablet per gallon of wine.

Top off the carboy with extra juice or sugar syrup (page 18), reinstall the airlock and if possible, store the carboy of wine in a cool, dark location for about two months and rack again, then rack again in a couple of months if necessary.

On to bottling, see page 23, 24. For bottling procedure see page 98-99.

MEAD

ONE GALLON

3 pounds clover honey
1/4 teaspoon grape tannin
3 teaspoons acid blend
2 teaspoon yeast nutrient powder
1 campden tablet, crush and dissolve
3 and 1/2 quarts of water
1 package Pasteur champagne yeast

Mix all ingredients (except the yeast) into the primary fermenter. Let stand overnight.

(See instructions for yeast starter on page 93.)

Add yeast starter, and stir. Fermentation should be noticeable in a day or two. In five or six days when fermentation has slowed down, rack and transfer to secondary fermenter.

(See secondary fermentation on page 95 through page 98).

If you like a sweeter wine, add Sorbistat K and the amount of sugar syrup needed for your taste, at bottling time.

ORANGE WINE

ONE GALLON

12 oz. frozen orange juice, or 10 to 12
 oranges
1 pound raisins
2 and 1/2 pounds cane sugar
1/2 teaspoon pectic enzyme powder
1/2 teaspoon acid blend
1 teaspoon yeast nutrient powder
1 package all purpose wine yeast
1 campden tablet, crush and dissolve
1 gallon water

Chop or mince the raisins.
Peel and chop the oranges.

If you like a sweeter wine, add Sorbistat K
and the amount of sugar syrup needed for your
taste, at bottling time.

Methodology: see page 91 through 98.

PEAR WINE

ONE GALLON

4 pounds ripe pears
Sugar, add sugar until hydrometer reading
is 1.095
1-1/2 teaspoon pectic enzyme
1 teaspoon yeast nutrient powder
1-1/2 teaspoon acid blend
1 campden tablet, crush and dissolve
1 package all purpose wine yeast
1 gallon water

Wash the pears, cut, remove the core and
chop the pears into small pieces, then crush.

If you like a sweeter wine, add Sorbistat K,
and the amount of sugar syrup needed for your
taste, at bottling time.

THREE GALLONS

12 pounds ripe pears
Sugar, add sugar until hydrometer reading
is 1.095
4 teaspoons pectic enzyme
3 teaspoons yeast nutrient powder
4 teaspoons acid blend
3 campden tablets, crush and dissolve
1 package all purpose wine yeast
3 gallons water

Procedure, same as above.
Methodology: see page 91 through 98.

PUMPKIN WINE

ONE GALLON

5 pounds pumpkin
6 cups brown sugar,
or 2 and 1/2 pounds cane sugar
2-1/2   teaspoons acid blend
1 teaspoon yeast nutrient powder
1/4 teaspoon grape tannin
1 campden tablet, crush and dissolve
1 package all purpose wine yeast
1 gallon water

Cut and remove the pumpkin skin, seeds and strings. Cut the pumpkin into small pieces. Put the pieces in a pan and mash. Pour the mashed pumpkin and juice into the primary fermenter.

Methodology: see page 91 through 98.

RAISIN WINE

ONE GALLON

2 pounds raisins, light or dark
2 pounds cane sugar, or a starting
specific gravity reading of 1.095
4 teaspoons acid blend
1 teaspoon yeast nutrient powder
1 campden tablet, crush and dissolve
1 package all purpose wine yeast
1 gallon water

Chop raisins, or use a coarse mincer.

THREE GALLONS

6 pounds raisins, light or dark
6 pound cane sugar, or a starting specific
gravity reading of 1.095
12 teaspoons acid blend
3 teaspoons yeast nutrient powder
3 campden tablets, crush and dissolve
1 package all purpose wine yeast
3 gallons water

Chop raisins, or use a coarse mincer

Methodology: See page 91 through 98.

RHUBARB WINE

ONE GALLON

5 pounds rhubarb
3 pounds cane sugar
1/4 teaspoon grape tannin
1 teaspoon yeast nutrient powder
1 campden tablet, crush and dissolve
1 package all purpose wine yeast
1 gallon water

Use the stalk only, no leaves. Chop rhubarb in small pieces. Put the pieces of rhubarb in a straining bag, preferably nylon. Tie securely, place the bag in a pan and crush the rhubarb as much as possible. Now put the bag of crushed rhubarb and juice into the primary fermenter. Boil the sugar in enough water to dissolve it. Let it cool and pour it over the rhubarb. Add the crushed and dissolved campden tablet and stir. Let this mixture sit in the covered primary fermenter for at least a couple of days. Remove the bag of pulp and strain as much juice from it as possible into the fermenter. Discard the pulp. Add all other ingredients, including yeast starter.

See Yeast Starter, page 93.

Methodology: for rhubarb wine, page 91 through 98.

If you desire a sweeter wine, add Sorbistat K and the amount sugar syrup needed for your taste at bottling time. For 3 gallons, multiply all the ingredients, except yeast, by 3.

For five gallons, multiply all the ingredients, except yeast by 5.

One package of yeast will make 1 to 5 gallons.

ROSE HIP WINE

ONE GALLON

6 oz. dried rose hips, preferably red
8 oz. raisins
2 pounds cane sugar
3/4 teaspoon acid blend
1 teaspoon yeast nutrient powder
1 campden tablet, crush and dissolve
1 gallon water
1 package all purpose wine yeast
1 gallon hot water

Chop the raisins. Put into primary fermenter. Add all other ingredients (except yeast). Pour in hot water and stir.

Methodology: see page 91 through 98.

STRAWBERRY WINE

ONE GALLON

3-1/2 pounds strawberries
2 pounds cane sugar
1 teaspoon yeast nutrient powder
1 teaspoon acid blend
1/2 teaspoon pectic enzyme
1/4 teaspoon grape tannin
1 campden tablet, crush and dissolve
1 package all purpose wine yeast
1 gallon water

Use only good, ripe strawberries. Sort through the berries. Pick out any that are bad. Remove any leaves or stems. Crush the berries in a pan. Put the crushed berries and the juice into the primary fermenter. Heat enough water to cover the berries, add sugar. Pour in the hot water and stir until well mixed. Add the crushed and dissolved campden tablet, stir, and let the mixture (must) set overnight. Now add the rest of the ingredients, including the yeast starter. (See, yeast starter, page 93.)

3 GALLONS

10-1/2 pounds strawberries
6 pounds cane sugar
3 teaspoons yeast nutrient powder
3 teaspoons acid blend
1 and 1/2 teaspoons pectic enzyme
3/4 teaspoon grape tannin
3 campden tablets, crush and dissolve

1 package all purpose wine yeast
3 gallons water

Same procedure as above.

Methodology: page 91 through 98.

 Oak Crusher

Oak Wine Press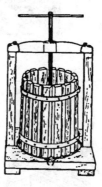

 American
White Oak
Barrels

8   The Vintager (Jost Amman) • Pruning the Vine (Aristide Maillol)

MAKING WINE VINEGAR
WITH
MOTHER OF VINEGAR CULTURE

You can make quality wine vinegar by using mother of vinegar culture.   Using the culture to make vinegar is very interesting, and for young people educational. You can watch the process in action, as the culture turns wine into vinegar.

Mother of vinegar culture can be purchased at most home wine and beermaking supply stores.

The ingredients and equipment needed are:

1. Mother of vinegar culture
2. Good, dry, red or white wine
3. Containers: Quart jars, wide mouth one gallon glass jars, or food grade plastic containers of various sizes, depending on amount of vinegar made.
4. Sanitizing solution, see page 75 -76 of this book.

Metal containers are not recommended due to the acid content of vinegar.

NOTE #1: If your water contains chlorine, draw the amount you need and let it stand, covered with a clean cloth for a day, or boil the water to reduce the amount of chlorine. Do this before staring your vinegar culture.

PROCEDURE: To start your vinegar, use ONE PART MOTHER OF VINEGAR CULTURE, ONE PART WATER and TWO PARTS DRY WINE. (Example--one pint mother of vinegar culture, one pint water, and two pints of wine.) When staring your vinegar, these proportions are important and should be followed closely. If you want to make one gallon or several gallons of wine vinegar, the procedure is basically the same.

Pour the vinegar culture, water and wine, into a clean, sanitized one gallon wide mouth container. Do not fill the container over three fourths full. Cover the top with a clean sanitized tight wove cloth, such as a piece of bed sheet, and tie securely. The cloth over the top, allows the mixture to breathe, as it needs as much air as possible while converting to vinegar. The cloth also keeps insects out of your culture. The container should then be stored in a warm area (70 to 80 degrees F).

NOTE # 2: The temperature where the working vinegar is kept should never exceed 90 degree F.

In two to four months, as you watch, a cap or "mother" will have formed on the top. The conversion from wine, water and culture to vinegar should be complete, and may be drawn off for use as vinegar.

Take a tablespoon full of vinegar. Put a sugar cube in it for a few seconds, take it out and chew the sugar cube. This way you will get the full flavor of the vinegar which will tell you if it is too weak, just right, or too strong.

If the vinegar is too weak, let it work for another week or so and test it again. If it is just right, use it. If it is too strong, dilute it with a little water, until you get the taste you want.

When you draw off any vinegar, the amount drawn off can be replaced with (two parts wine with 11% alcohol and one part water). If the alcohol content of your wine is around 9%, add only a little water. If the alcohol content of your wine is around 6%, as is some berry wine and hard cider, do not add any water.

If you want to increase the amount of vinegar you are making, and you have, for example, one gallon of finished vinegar; you can add one gallon of water and two gallons of wine to your vinegar.

After complete conversion of the vinegar culture to vinegar, if you choose, it may be filtered. It can also be pasteurized by filling your bottles with vinegar and heating the uncapped bottles in a pan of water. This takes about 30 minutes at 140 to 150 degrees F., and not more than 160 degrees F. When the bottles cool to about 70 degrees, cap or cork. This helps preserve the vinegar and give it a smoother, pleasing taste as it ages.

CAUTION: If you make your own wine, and you also want to make vinegar, it would be best not to make them at the same time, or store them in the same area. It would also be a good idea not to make them in the same building. The vinegar spores can get into your wine before it is bottled, and spoil your wine.

For a complete up-to-date book on making homemade vinegar, get a copy of:

HOMEMADE WINE VINEGAR
made with
MOTHER OF VINEGAR

CONVERSION TABLE

1 Gallon = 4 quarts = 8 pints = 128 ounces

1 Quart = 2 pints = 4 cups = 32 ounces

1 Pint = 2 cups = 32 tablespoons = 16 ounces

1 Cup = 16 tablespoons = 48 teaspoons = 8 ounces

1 Fluid ounce = 2 tablespoons = 6 teaspoons

1/2 Fluid ounce = 1 tablespoon = 3 teaspoons

3 Teaspoons = 1 tablespoon

1/2 of 1/4 Teaspoon = 1/8 teaspoon

1 Pound = 16 ounces

1/2 Pound = 8 ounces

1/4 Pound = 4 ounces

1/8 Pound = 2 ounces

CONVERSION FACTORS

To convert from	To	Multiply by
Cups	ounces	8.0
Gallons	liters	3.79
Grams	milligrams	1000
Grams	ounces	0.035
Kilograms	grams	1000
Kilograms	ounces	35.27
Kilograms	pounds	2.2
Liters	gallons	0.264
Liters	ounces	33.8
Liters	pints	2.11
Liters	quarts	1.06
Ounces	grams	28.3
Pints	gallon	0.125
Pints	ounces	16
Pounds	grams	453.6
Quarts	liters	0.946
Tablespoons	ounces	0.5
Tablespoons	milliliters	15
Teaspoons	milliliters	5
Teaspoons	tablespoons	3

INDEX

WINE RECIPES

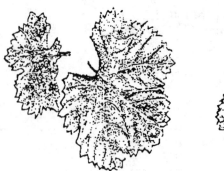

WHERE TO OBTAIN SUPPLIES

Home wine and beermaking supply stores!

Look in the yellow pages of your phone book, or of a large city nearby. A store may be listed under wine or beermaking supplies.

If you cannot locate a home wine and beermaking supply store in your area. Write to:

A - Printing Co.
Post Office Box 5523
Napa CA 94581
Telephone (707) 255-6408

A - Printing Co. will refer your letter to a home wine and beermaking supply store that will send you a free catalog. The catalog will contain the supplies you will need for making homemade wine and beer.

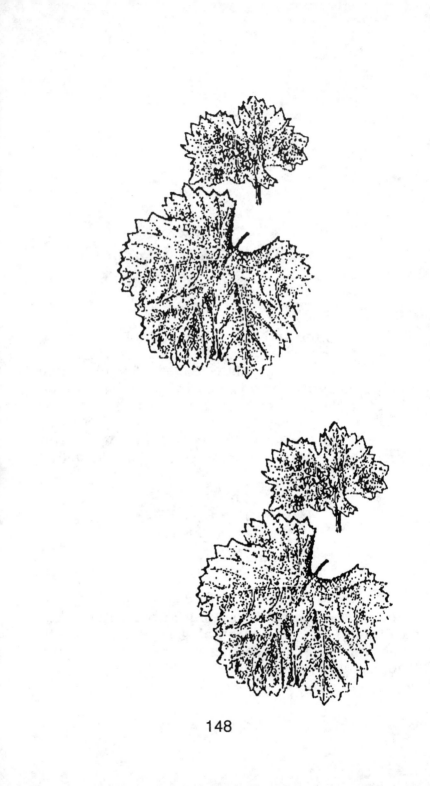

NOTES ON MAKING WINE

NOTES ON MAKING WINE

NOTES ON MAKING WINE

MORE NOTES ON MAKING WINE

MORE NOTE ON WINEMAKING

MORE NOTES ON WINEMAKING

NOTES ON MAKING HOMEMADE VINEGAR

MORE NOTES ON MAKING HOMEMADE VINEGAR

A-Printing Co. Post Office Box 5523   **ORDER FORM**
Napa, CA 94581 / or call (707) 255-6408

Please send me the following books:

_____Homemade Wine Vinegar / made with
      Mother of Vinegar $ 6.95 each.
      by Patrick and Carole Watkins 1995

_____Jim and George's Home Winemaking
      A Beginner's Book by Jim Weathers $ 6.95 each.
      revised and updated 1995

_____Practical Beermaking / A Beginner's
      Book by Jim Weathers $ 6.95 each.
      revised and updated 1995

                     Sub Total_____

         Calif. Residents add sales tax_____

                    Shipping_____

                        Total_____

Name:_____

Address:_____

City:_____State_____Zip_____

Shipping:
$ 2.25 for first book, .75 cents for each additional book.

_____I do not want to wait 3-4 weeks for my book(s)
sent book rate. Here is $ 3.50 per book for First Class Mail.

Prices subject to change

158

A-Printing Co. Post Office Box 5523   **ORDER FORM**
Napa, CA 94581 / or call (707) 255-6408

Please send me the following books:

_____Homemade Wine Vinegar / made with
      Mother of Vinegar $ 6.95 each.
      by Patrick and Carole Watkins 1995

_____Jim and George's Home Winemaking
      A Beginner's Book by Jim Weathers $ 6.95 each.
      revised and updated 1995

_____Practical Beermaking / A Beginner's
      Book by Jim Weathers $ 6.95 each.
      revised and updated 1995

                    Sub Total_____

        Calif. Residents add sales tax_____

                        Shipping_____

                          Total_____

Name:_____

Address:_____

City:_____State_____Zip_____

Shipping:
$ 2.25 for first book, .75 cents for each additional book.

_____I do not want to wait 3-4 weeks for my book(s)
sent book rate. Here is $ 3.50 per book for First Class Mail.

Prices subject to change